PLAYS
MEGAN TERRY

BROADWAY PLAY PUBLISHING INC
56 E 81st St., NY NY 10028-0202
212 772-8334 fax: 212 772-8358
http://www.BroadwayPlayPubl.com

PLAYS BY MEGAN TERRY

First printing: December 2000
I S B N: 0-88145-185-1

Book design: Marie Donovan
Word processing: Microsoft Word for Windows
Typographic controls: Xerox Ventura Publisher 2.0 P E
Typeface: Palatino
Copy editing: Sue Gilad
Printed on recycled acid-free paper and bound in the U S A

CONTENTS

ABOUT THE AUTHOR

Some of Megan Terry's other plays include BREAKFAST SERIAL, CALM DOWN MOTHER, KEEP TIGHTLY CLOSED IN A COOL DRY PLACE, HOTHOUSE, EX-MISS COPPER QUEEN ON A SET OF PILLS, THE PEOPLE VS RANCHMAN, GOONA GOONA, MOLLIE BAILEY'S TRAVELING FAMILY CIRCUS: FEATURING SCENES FROM THE LIFE OF MOTHER JONES, PRO GAME, BODY LEAKS, SOUND FIELDS, and OBJECTIVE LOVE. She has published over forty-five plays; most have been translated and produced world wide.

She has won all the major writing awards, including a Guggenheim, and received an Obie award for APPROACHING SIMONE. She was elected to lifetime membership by the College of Fellows of the American Theatre (installation at the Kennedy Center, Washington, DC) in recognition of: "Distinguished service to the profession by an individual of acknowledged national stature." In 1992 she was named Nebraska Artist of the Year. Terry is photographer and co-editor of *Right Brain Vacation Photos, New Plays and Production Photographs 1972-1992.*

Ms Terry has a degree from the University of Washington, certificates in acting, directing and design from the Banff School of Fine Arts, Banff, Alberta, Canada, and was awarded the Yale-A B C Fellowship, "Writing for the Camera", at Yale University.

Currently, Megan Terry, is editing the Omaha Magic Theatre archives along with hundreds of her videotapes and photographs. Terry is at work on a new play, BOUNCE, and is preparing final versions of her work STAR PATH MOON STOP. She is playwright in residence, photographer, performer and musician at the Omaha Magic Theatre, Omaha, Nebraska.

INTRODUCTION

These three plays are special to me because they have a life of their own. When I was working on them, my main thought was to make them strong enough to work for the audiences of that time. Each was written from a passionate position. VIET ROCK, was forged with the single minded purpose to make one more contribution to STOP that war. The fact that it was the first full-length transformation play and the first Rock Musical is the result of content dictating form. The war seemed to be fought in the media and in American streets as well as on the ground and in the air of South East Asia. The talent, imagination and power of those of the Open Theatre who worked on the play was awesome. The composer, Marianne de Pury, attended every workshop and wrote the score as we developed the piece. We had no money for lavish production, but we felt the technique, power and presence of the actors to create a multitude of characters and places via the acting technique of transformation was all the production value we needed at that time. The Artistic Director of the Open Theatre, Joseph Chaikin, had brought these actors to a heroic point of performance expression. Almost immediately after its initial performances, theatre companies the world over and in many American universities produced the play. They had reconstructed it according to their attitudes and their special gifts as a company. I have a file cabinet full of correspondence, photos and reviews ranging from Tokyo to Ohio State University from theater people who bonded with one another, their audiences and with us through the experience of their work on the material of this piece.

When I was with the Open Theatre and then The Omaha Magic Theatre we always played the nearby prison for free when we played a touring date at a university or another theater company. Out of ten years of interviews, close contact and observation of incarcerated people in both male and female prisons, from maximum security to minimum to the constantly manacled but communicative criminally insane, I created the play along with the powerful director-performer Jo Ann Schmidman, Artistic Director of the Omaha Magic Theatre. We had met many "political" prisoners in our travels and we were almost constantly accosted on streets by police ourselves. At that time, if one was not carrying an I D they would throw you in the nearest jail for "vagrancy". Many times we had to bail out our actors just in time to make the opening curtain of a show. We decided to make this piece to learn how to survive ourselves in "the system". We also saw it as a metaphor for the plight of women and others in an overbearing patriarchal culture. We had as many men as women in the company and the men wanted to play women, to explore what it was like to be a woman at that point in time, not from a camp perspective but finding the woman in themselves to project. A side result from this mixed cast of women and men, all playing women, was that many men in audiences all over the U S (we toured the play for three years) came to us after the play to say, "At last I'm beginning to understand what women are talking about. I identified with the men playing women and I was revolted and horrified to think, what if I had been born a woman and had to accept that role prescribed for me by others?"

APPROACHING SIMONE is very special to me because her work is a never-ending influence. I collected articles, books, fragments of her work and the work of others about her life and work over a period of fifteen years. I felt a deep, urgent necessity for a spiritual education. I'm still going to school to learn about Simone. I had chanced upon one sentence she said in a magazine and the depth of how her words hit me sent me on the quest. I believe she is one of the most profound theological thinkers of the last hundred years. She made the effort to leave us fifteen books, none published in her lifetime. She is an exemplary model of the one who gives one's wholehearted being for the enlightenment of others. I believe she was killed in action while in service to her beloved France.

"If God had given me more than one life, I would have spent one of them with you."
Simone Weil

ACKNOWLEDGMENTS

Megan Terry wishes to thank the Rockefeller Foundation and their representatives, Arthur Ballet, Norman Lloyd, William Bradley, Howard Klein, and Susan Sato, who early on believed in my work and supported me through the years with money and encouragement. I also thank The National Endowment for the Arts, The Nebraska Arts Council and N A C Executive Director, Jennifer Severin, The Guggenheim Foundation, The Lila Wallace Readers Digest Foundation, and the incomparable and generous Ellen Stewart, who got my "beeps" and produced many of my pieces at her famed Café LaMama. I'm deeply grateful to Joseph Chaikin and the Open Theatre Members for all their great, groundbreaking work and inspiration; and to composer Marianne de Pury, who wrote the rock music score for VIET ROCK. I want to thank Richard Schechner for being first to publish my work and then talking Simon and Schuster into bringing out four of my plays. Thanks, too, to Robert Brustein for his counsel and for producing VIET ROCK at Yale, and to Richard Gilman for his insight and for "needling" me into writing full-length works. And special thanks to Jordan Charney, Nancy Cooperstein, and the exceptional David Rothenberg for their courage in bringing VIET ROCK to Off Broadway. I want to thank Boston University for commissioning me to write APPROACHING SIMONE as part of the celebration of their centennial, and I'm deeply appreciative of the work of the Omaha Magic Theatre Company for their dedication in realizing the production of BABES IN THE BIGHOUSE, and to the outstanding and innovative composer, John J Sheehan and the brilliant Artistic Director, Jo Ann Schmidman, an awesome and tireless director/collaborator and a powerful, outstanding performer. And, finally words are inadequate to express my gratitude and devotion to the memory of my agent, Elisabeth Marton, and her no-nonsense attitude. Her personal integrity and the beauty of her soul and person guided me. Her niece, Tonda Marton, carries on in her spirit.

APPROACHING SIMONE

for Jo Ann Schmidman

ORIGINAL PRODUCTION

APPROACHING SIMONE was commissioned and first presented by The Division of Theater Arts of the School of Fine and Applied Arts In Celebration of Boston Universitys Centennial, opening on 25 February 1970, at Boston University Theater, 264 Huntington Avenue, Boston, Massachusetts. The cast and creative contributors were:

THE COMPANY:

Erica Applesweig
Francesca Bartoccini
Zelda Batt
Faith Catlin
Edward M D'Amiata
Paula Duesing
Ronald Eddo
Jackie Elliot
Philip Fisher
Gina Fitzhugh
Pete Gallatin
Deborah Goss
Liebe Gray
Michael Griggs
Helen Hoffman
Edward P Howes
Leslie L Hurley
Chris Kapalo
Stephen Klein
David Carlton Kneuss
Geraldine Librandi
Susan McLeod
Mary Ellen Meade
Rick Minichiello
Robert Osolinski
Peggy Pape
Louise M. Pesare
Christina Putnam
Helane S. Rosenberg
James Seymour
JoAnn Schmidman
James Sherwood
Michael Sirota
Lois Slembecker
Mychelle Smiley
Linda Spohn

Director .... Maxine Klein
Music composed & conducted by .... William S Fischer
Set designer .... John Kasard
Costume designer .... James Berton Harris
Light designer .... Sidney Bennett

Electric piano .... Michael Cochran
Acoustic piano .... Ross Dabrusin
Flute .... Dave Bruskin
Percussion .... Art Gore
Saxophone .... Larry Scripp
Trumpet .... Louis Siegal
Bass .... Paul Brinkey

The play then moved to New York City and opened on 4 March 1970, presented by La Mama Repertory Theater and Boston University School of Fine and Applied Arts, The Division of Theater Arts at 74A East 4th Street, with the above cast and creative contributors.

Author's note: "Simone" is to be played by one actor, while the rest of the ensemble transforms to other characters and/or objects.

CHARACTERS

SIMONE
FATHER
MOTHER
BROTHER
VISITOR
SIMONE *(a college friend of* SIMONE'*s)*
ALBERT
JEAN-PAUL
CAROLINA
BOARD HEAD 1
BOARD HEAD 2
FRENCH MILITARY MEN *(played by the same actor)*
THE ENSEMBLE
QUEENS
KINGS

Production note: No specific music is available. The music is up to the discretion of each individual director.

ACT ONE

(The stage of the proscenium opening should be raked at a high enough angle so that any floor movement or choreography can be seen from anywhere in the house. Throughout the auditorium may be five small platforms, covering the theater seats, with stairs or ropes or bridges for the actors to reach them. There is a balcony stage left and another stage right where the opera singers will stand and sing in spotlights when necessary. Coming out from the proscenium opening on both stage right and stage left are two platforms against the house walls, wide enough to hold ornate chairs and from four to eight actors each. On stage right platform, which should be lower than the height of the main stage but high enough that the audience can see heads and shoulders, are male actors, dressed in the costumes of kings, emperors, presidents, prelates, etc. They are all very old. On stage left platform jutting out from the proscenium are female actors dressed in haute couture of the thirties. They are anybody's idea of society and culture leaders. They are very old. Draped above the proscenium opening are the intermingled flags of France, Nazi Germany, Russia, England, and the United States. In the center of the flags is a giant icon, painted in muted, glowing colors and illuminated with gold leaf, of God in a flowing white beard at the top, Jesus below and to the left, a golden glow below and to the right.)

(In the corners of the proscenium arch where the arch and the walls of the house join, stage right and stage left, are papier-mâché cherubs painted in gold. They stand from floor to ceiling. In their belly buttons are golden rings: to the rings are attached golden cords. The cords are held by the old men and old women and will be pulled at the appropriate time.)

(On the ceiling is a beautiful head with an open mouth. The company enters from back of the auditorium in procession. As they reach the stage, they turn and face the audience. The woman who plays SIMONE *takes up position at extreme stage left and silently stares at the audience. The company sings.)*

ALL: The darkness, the darkness
I'm not afraid of the night
The darkness, the darkness
Where I groped inside
I loved the light on the snow
I sent my sugar to the war
I watched good Frenchmen
Go
Into the ground
But I paid attention to the sound

Of the pounding dark
Within my head
I followed where the heartbeat led
And my mind seemed to bleed.

BARITONE: If the fool persists in his folly
He will become wise
If the fool persists in his folly
He will become wise.

Desire! Desire! Desire! Desire!
Ecstasy! Mind ecstasy! Desire!
Desire!

Eclipse the fire of the sexual drive
Reach out through the mind
Leave the sperm behind
Let the egg fall where she may
Drive, drive, drive
To mind ecstasy.

(The CHORUS *keeps singing, "Attention, Attention.")*

WOMAN: Anyone can become
Anyone can become

MAN: Anyone can know truth
Anyone can know truth

ALL: Desire! Desire!

DUET: Only make the effort of attention
Only make the effort of attention
Stay in the dark inside your head
(Repeat)
Till it lights your way.

ALL: Attention, pull with your will.
Genius is invisible.

(One by one everyone sings the name "Simone" on a different note, then everyone taking her or his same note sings the name "Simone" five times together.)

ACTOR: *(Intones from platform)* Simone taught herself the art of perpetual attention. Simone taught herself the art of perpetual attention. *(Exit)*

(No matter what age SIMONE *is during a scene, she always behaves and speaks as if she were somewhere near thirty.)*

*(*SIMONE *enters running and flings herself down. Her family follows. They mime carrying luggage.)*

MOTHER: Get up, Simone. We have a long way to walk to the lodge.

SIMONE: I have nothing to carry.

MOTHER: You're too little.

FATHER: You don't have to carry anything.

BROTHER: You can't carry anything, you're only five.

SIMONE: I can carry anything.

MOTHER: Get up at once.

SIMONE: I can carry as much as Brother.

FATHER: My dear little girl. Father can carry you and the luggage too: climb on my back.

SIMONE: I want to carry my share.

MOTHER: There's no need.

BROTHER: You're melting the snow.

MOTHER: You'll catch pneumonia.

FATHER: T B.

BROTHER: I'm starving. Come on, Simone.

SIMONE: No.

MOTHER: Simone.

SIMONE: No.

FATHER: Simone.

SIMONE: No.

MOTHER: You'll get bronchitis, you'll get the flu, you'll have a headache, your clothes will be wet. You'll not sleep a wink. I won't sleep a wink. I'll be up all night with you coughing. You're too frail. You were not only ill all this fall but you were in bed most of the summer. Please, my little darling, come now and take Mama's hand.

SIMONE: No. I can carry as much as he can.

BROTHER: Let's see.

*(*SIMONE *stands up and* BROTHER *mimes transference of luggage on his back to* SIMONE*'s back. She wobbles, gets her balance, and slowly trudges ahead.)*

MOTHER: What will we do with her, she'll break her bones before she's six.

FATHER: Let her have her way. She can't keep it up.

BROTHER: *(Running off)* I will eat all the croissants.

*(*MOTHER *and* FATHER *freeze.)*

(This series of scenes should be played very quickly in different pools of light.)

*(*BROTHER *and* SIMONE*)*

BROTHER: Do you know your Racine?

SIMONE: Of course.

BROTHER: Then whoever dries up first gets slapped by the other.

(He begins to recite Phaedra. *He stumbles.* SIMONE *slaps him and continues the passage. She falters and he slaps her.)*

BROTHER: Continue.

*(*SIMONE *continues to recite; she gets slapped twice.)*

BROTHER: Continue. Continue.

*(*VISITOR, MOTHER, BROTHER, SIMONE*)*

BROTHER: I solved all the math problems before the teacher could.

MOTHER: He's been first in his class in everything since he started school.

VISITOR: He's the genius, and *(Pointing to* SIMONE*)* she's the beauty.

*(*SIMONE *turns away as if slapped by an invisible hand.)*

*(*SIMONE, BROTHER, *and* MOTHER*)*

MOTHER: My dearest children, where are your stockings?

BROTHER: We gave them away.

MOTHER: It's raining and freezing out.

SIMONE: The workers' children don't wear stockings, and neither do I!

MOTHER: I won't permit this. Your father won't permit this. You're not to leave the house till I send out for more stockings.

SIMONE: I will never wear stockings again.

*(*SIMONE *and* MOTHER. SIMONE *is pouring sugar into an envelope.)*

MOTHER: My precious baby, my own, my darling, what are you doing with that precious sugar? It was so hard for me to get. I had the maid stand in line three hours for it.

SIMONE: I'm mailing my sugar to the soldiers at the front.

MOTHER: But why?

SIMONE: They don't have any.

(At the beach: FATHER *and* SIMONE. SIMONE *is gazing at the sunset. The* ENSEMBLE *becomes waves, gulls, shore birds, etc.)*

FATHER: Simone, you've been sitting looking out over the water for hours—go and play with the other children.

SIMONE: It's so beautiful. I'd much rather watch the sunset than play.

(She screams a long agonized scream. The ENSEMBLE *rush upstage and turn with their mouths open in mirror agony.)*

SIMONE: Father, I have an impossible headache. I've never never known such pain. It's driving me out of my mind.

FATHER: It's probably connected to your menstrual cycle. This often happens the first few times.

SIMONE: It's not like ordinary pain. I'm going blind. I'm afraid I'll vomit.

FATHER: *(Feeling her forehead)* You don't have a fever. Where's the pain centered?

SIMONE: It started in my left eye and now has traveled to the right. I can't stand the light. I can't stand the noise. The noise in the street is trampling on my brain.

FATHER: Sounds like migraine. I hope not, my precious child. Go and lie down in your room. I'll bring an ice cloth for your head, and make it very dark until you feel better. *(Exit)*

*(*SIMONE *at Fourteen—When and Why She Wants to Kill Herself)*

*(*SIMONE *is alone in her room with the wet cloth. As her pain and anguish build, aspects of her self-doubt, self-loathing, and pain appear to torture her. Each one brings a larger and larger piece of white wet cloth until she is all wrapped up except for her head, with a piece left to strangle herself [or one giant white cloth can be used].)*

SIMONE: Oh Father, Father, it's unbearable. Surely it's some kind of punishment.

ONE: You have no talent, Simone.

TWO: You're stupid, Simone.

THREE: You're awkward, Simone.

FOUR: Not only is your body miserable, but your mind can't move either.

FIVE: You're nothing but a girl, Simone.

SIX: You'll never amount to anything, Simone.

SEVEN: You'll never match your brother, Simone.

EIGHT: You're only a girl, Simone.

(Taunts from the auditorium in three languages, equivalent to "You're nothing but a stupid cunt")

NINE: The pain in your head is evidence.

TEN: Evidence of your lack of brains, Simone.

ELEVEN: You'll never know the truth, Simone.

TWELVE: Your mind is too dim to perceive the truth, Simone.

THIRTEEN: Put an end to your stupidity, Simone.

FOURTEEN: Beauty is useless, Simone; it isn't the path to the truth.

FIFTEEN: You're unworthy, Simone.

SIXTEEN: You're wretched, Simone.

SEVENTEEN: You're unfit for this world, Simone.

EIGHTEEN: You're arrogant, Simone.

NINETEEN: You'll never create anything, Simone.

TWENTY: You have no talent, Simone.

TWENTY-ONE: You have no genius, Simone.

TWENTY-TWO: You're a girl, Simone.

TWENTY- THREE: Your pain is your proof, Simone.

TWENTY-FOUR: You're always sick and you'll always be sick, Simone.

TWENTY-FIVE: Your head will always ache, Simone.

TWENTY-SIX: You can't even draw a straight line, Simone.

TWENTY-SEVEN: You have poor circulation, Simone.

TWENTY-EIGHT: Your hands are always swollen, Simone.

TWENTY-NINE: It takes brains to discover the truth, Simone.

SIMONE: If I can't find the way to justice and truth, then I don't want to live! I'm mediocre! Only the truly great can enter that transcendant kingdom where truth lives.

THIRTY: Kill yourself, Simone.

*(*THIRTY *unrolls the white sheet* SIMONE *rolls tortuously out. As the* SINGER *sings,* SIMONE *is drawn back to the will to live. She slowly rises.)*

SINGER: Anyone can know truth
Desire, desire
Only make the effort of attention
Focus on the dark inside your head
Until it lights your way
The simplest man may know truth
If he reaches out every day

(A nightclub. SIMONE *sits smoking buried behind the menu. Her friends* SIMONE, JEAN-PAUL, ALBERT, *and some others sit around tables. There is a small band playing in the background.)*

SIMONE TWO: Simone, roll me a cigarette.

JEAN-PAUL: She's too clumsy.

ALBERT: She's getting better.

SIMONE TWO: They burn longer—she packs them tight.

JEAN-PAUL: Simone, your lips.

SIMONE: Eh?

ALBERT: You're reading the script off the menu.

JEAN-PAUL: She won't order anything anyway.

ALBERT: I'll order for her. Tonight we eat.

JEAN-PAUL: Tonight we drink. Whiskey!

SIMONE TWO: Whiskey! Whiskey, Simone?

SIMONE: No.

SIMONE TWO: Here, take my tobacco.

SIMONE: Thanks.

JEAN-PAUL: *(Watching* SIMONE *roll cigarette)* Hey, she's doing it with one hand.

ALBERT: American.

SIMONE: TWO: Twist the end, like yours. Ah.

*(*SIMONE*, rolling cigarettes in each hand, drops them and gets tobacco all over her skirt, the table. She tries to brush it together. Everyone sputters.)*

JEAN-PAUL: Get it out of the way. Carolina is almost on.

SIMONE: TWO: We were lucky to get in.

ALBERT: I'm in love with her.

SIMONE: How long has she been in France?

ALBERT: I hope she never leaves; she's promised never to leave.

SIMONE: I'd like to talk with her sometime.

(Her friends laugh. Successfully rolling another cigarette for herself, she lights it with the stub of the one in her mouth.)

SIMONE: They've been so exploited. We do the same in our colonies. How can you sit here drinking and grinning like apes when we are grinding down the blacks in Africa?

JEAN-PAUL: We'll change all that tomorrow. Tonight we have fun.

SIMONE: TWO: Simone is right. Have you written a position paper on the colonies?

JEAN-PAUL: I will, I will. I have to form a coalition with the workers first.

ALBERT: It won't be hard. The monetary system is cracking. I predict within six months, a year at most, we'll have no trouble recruiting.

JEAN-PAUL: The international capitalistic beast has fed on itself so long, it won't find even a kernel of corn left in its shit to keep it going.

SIMONE: It's beginning to happen in Germany. I plan to go there to examine the new workers' alliances at first hand.

JEAN-PAUL: I'll publish anything you send back.

SIMONE: Good. but I won't have much time to write. I intend to work.

ALBERT: Work, work. Always work. Whiskey!

SIMONE: Everything begins and ends with work. Work is constant. You and I pass through, but the work is always here.

SIMONE: TWO: One day machines will do all the work.

SIMONE: If we are not careful, we will work for the machines.

JEAN-PAUL: Technology will free man from manual labor.

SIMONE: I hope not.

ALBERT: What is so sacred about working with your hands. I've never worked with my hands and I never intend to—we're freed from that.

SIMONE: You are privileged; they are not.

ALBERT: I want to think; I want to plan, create.

SIMONE: You above all should understand work. Work, in contrast to reflection, to persuasion or to magic, is a sequence of actions that have no direct connection either with the initial emotion, or the end aimed at.... Colors, sounds, dimensions can change, while the law of work, which is to be endlessly indifferent to what has preceded and what will follow, never changes. Qualities, forms, and distances change, but the law of work remains the constant factor to which qualities, forms, and distances serve only as signs. The law of exterior relations defines space. To see space is to grasp that work's raw material is always passive, always outside one's self.

ALBERT: Whiskey.

SIMONE: TWO: Here she comes.

JEAN-PAUL: Simone. Attend her closely. Tell me if Carolina is working or creating magic.

SIMONE: *(Smoking again, she sits back.)* Now you 're working too hard, Jean-Paul.

WAITER: Caro-lin-A!!

*(*CAROLINA, *an African-American entertainer, takes the stage. She sings first in a blues style that changes to a Charleston and then back to a shoutin' blues. She's backed by a mixed chorus who dance in the style of 1928–29.)*

CAROLINA: *(Singing and dancing, blues, Charleston, tap, stomp)*:
The blues was a pass time
The blues was a pass time
For that time
I didn't have no time
For nothin' but the blues

I could spend the day
I could lay there all the day
Passin' time with my blues

The blues was my pass time
That was the last time that I
Let the blues get me that way

My latest old man left me in bed
He walked on down to the store
He'd watched my red heart
Turn to lead
He said "chile, chile, chile,
I jes cain't sleep with you no more."
It's past time for the blues
They don't gonna grab me no more
I ain't layin' with the blues
I'm sick of the heartsick
I done licked the blues
It's long past time for the blues
My red heart done turned to blue
But along came a pretty man
Who made me know my eyes was black
He tole me, Baby, you is mine now and
Yore old man ain't never comin back
And I'm glad he's gone
Oh yes, I'm glad he's gone
I got a new man, not a blue man
He gives me sugar at night
He gives me sugar at night
He bakes my bread
He holds me tight
He calls me his peaches
I calls him my cream
He creams
My peaches
He creams my peaches,

And Baby let me tell you,
Baby let me tell you,
This ain't no dream!!

(They applaud wildly, bang the table; ALBERT *jumps up and invites her to the table. She comes over and he introduces her around. She shakes hands.* SIMONE *crunches down in her chair. She is very shy, lights two cigarettes at once, and starts to pick up the menu again. The band begins a mild Charleston.* CAROLINA *bends over* SIMONE.*)*

CAROLINA: Hello baby, give me some sugar. Hey baby, give me some sugar.

(As SIMONE *turns red,* CAROLINA *kisses her on the neck, and then pulls her to her feet.)*

CAROLINA: Come on and Charleston, Charleston with me.

SIMONE: I beg your pardon?

CAROLINA: Dance, baby.

SIMONE: I don't know how.

CAROLINA: Follow me.

*(*SIMONE *hands notebook to* ALBERT*)*

SIMONE: I'm afraid....

CAROLINA: Don't work so hard...like this, nice and easy does it...

*(*SIMONE, *awkward, makes some attempt. Her friends are delighted.)*

SIMONE: I can't get my hands right.

CAROLINA: You'll get it, you'll get it. Let it come up through the floor. Let it creep right up ya spine. Yeah, yeah, you gettin' it. Who's buyin'?

ALBERT: *(Yelling)* Whiskey.

JEAN-PAUL: Work or magic, Simone?

SIMONE: It's divine, Jean-Paul.

(They all laugh.)

ALBERT: So are you. What do you drink, Carolina?

CAROLINA: Old Forrester, neat.

(As they exit:)

ALBERT: Say you will never leave France. Say you will never leave me.

CAROLINA: Anything you say, baby—it's really true what they said about Paree.

*(*SIMONE *remains alone onstage. The ensemble appears in grotesque gray bags. They move slowly to smother her. She remains in one place.)*

SIMONE: *(A litany)* What I am, I endure. What I am, I endure. I suffer, I desire, I doubt, I'm stupid. I'm ignorant, I'm not well put together. What I am does not satisfy me. I have become me without my consent. Tomorrow is an I that now I cannot change. What I am, I endure, I suffer.

(The ensemble covers her for an instant then break and dissolve upstage. Alone:)

SIMONE: I desire, I am stupid! What I am, I endure.

(SIMONE and her MOTHER arrive in a truck made of the ensemble at the rooms where SIMONE's first teaching post is to be. SIMONE is chain smoking and reading newspapers and magazines throughout the scene. The truck is loaded with all sorts of furniture, etc. The MOTHER directs two workmen who mime unloading and placing the articles. SIMONE sits, reads, and makes rapid notes.)

MOTHER: A delightful cottage. Looks tight. I shall check for drafts. Bring in the furniture.

(SIMONE takes a fast glance and goes back to her reading; the minute a chair is placed she sits and continues.)

MOTHER: The bed there, the photos there, the commode there, the bureau there, the table there, the chairs here, the sofa there, the rug here, no the bed here out of the draft; now the rug back here, the bureau there, the desk here.

(She pays movers. They exit.)

MOTHER: Simone, see the view from your desk. You'll be able to correct your papers while you watch the sun set. Be sure not to open the window when you work: it gives you pain in your neck. We'll all miss you and write every week. Take possession of your pupils; they're lucky to have you. I've furnished your room. It's beautiful. See how well everything fits. Be well and happy and write every week. Do you like what I've done?

SIMONE: *(Taking cigarette out of her mouth)* It's beautiful, darling.

MOTHER: You must keep well and let me know the minute anything happens. Don't catch cold, and try to remember to eat. Promise me you'll remember to eat.

SIMONE: I promise, my darling mother, and I promise I'll write you both every week.

(MOTHER kisses SIMONE, then exits. SIMONE starts to speak but lights another cigarette and methodically rounds up all the furniture except desk, chair, and bed and pushes them over into the orchestra pit. Then she goes to sleep on the floor.)

(Lights dim a moment—then come up bright morning. Her first class of girls is entering, chattering, and wondering about their new teacher.)

ALL: *Bonjour. (Et cetera)*

(SIMONE rises and waves her hand at them without looking; she is deep in thought.)

PUPIL: *Does that mean we're supposed to sit down?*

(They push one another into the classroom, trying to suppress laughter and excitement. The men in the ensemble have assumed the position of desks. The girls each choose one and sit on his back.)

SIMONE: *(Pacing)* To teach or not to teach, that is the way to earn my bread. To teach or not to teach. That is the way to earn my soul. I hate to eat. What is feeding?

(During all this the girls are secretly looking at her, making fun of her, sizing her up, passing notes and making gestures.)

SIMONE: *Bonjour mes chers enfants. Bon.* It's a good day. Did you see the sunrise?

(Class giggles.)

SIMONE: It's good to get up in time to see the sunrise. You all do it. You have to get to school on time.

CLASS: *(Bored) Bonjour, Mademoiselle. (They turn off and look out at the audience and stay very stiff while shuffling their feet and picking their ears, or secretly scratching their crotches.)*

SIMONE: I have some new ideas.

(Many groans from class)

SIMONE: They will stimulate your minds.

(Many more groans and stamping of feet. SIMONE *walks around in agitation. Students watch her.)*

SIMONE: Listen to me. If you won't bend a little, I'll have to smoke.

(Class laughs and claps.)

SIMONE: I'm fighting off lighting up a cigarette, because I'm trying to teach you.

CLASS: *(Sighs, mocking)* Ohhh!

SIMONE: I've been educated in Paris.

CLASS: *(Sighs)* Oooo!

SIMONE: I've been educated by the bourgeoisie to teach you to be like me, and if that is what you want, that is what you'll get.

STUDENT: We knew that before we came. That's why we're here. How else will we get good jobs?

SIMONE: At the same time that I teach you to be like what your parents expect, because I too love and respect my parents and wish to live up to what they respect, I do wish to make some innovations.

CLASS: Not another innovation.

SIMONE: What I as a teacher would like to do with my life is to try to work out with you as I'm working out with myself some of the things important to all of us. Since this class is concerned with the philosophy syllabus, what I'd like to do is to demonstrate to you how philosophy came into being as a name, as a way of thinking; I want you to know the history and the definition of it and not just the name "philosophy" that will be found one day written in your exercise books. I care to speak to you about how to live.

STUDENT: *(Laughs)* But we're already alive.

SIMONE: Everywhere?

STUDENT: Where's that.

SIMONE: That is what we'll discover. Class dismissed for today.

(Girls rise and exit—talking bewilderedly—then return. As they enter the classroom again, they push their desks closer to SIMONE.)

SIMONE: *Bonjour.*

CLASS: *Bonjour (Hi, hello, et cetera)*

SIMONE: Who wishes to hike this weekend?

(All raise hands, with exclamations.)

SIMONE: We're taking a difficult trail.

(Still all raise hands, make sounds of assurance.)

SIMONE: I think we'll have good weather, and I don't want to miss it before it gets too cold. I want you to begin to take yourselves more seriously as writers. It seems to me a good way to do this would be for you to see your work in print. Therefore, I've procured a printing press, and from now on all compositions in philosophy will be printed. This will mean extra hours because you'll have to learn how to run the printing press, but that will be a good lesson in physics and mathematics as it relates to work.

(Girls run out while men become a printing press. Girls slide down a ramp, into the press—men stamp them as girls triumphantly laugh and then run out to audience to read to them their bits of poems or philosophy. The actors should write or choose these things themselves [in the Boston production the actors chose lines from the works of Simone Weil]. Each girl finds several audience members to speak to. After girls have reached as many audience members as possible, they gather at back of auditorium and begin their hike—over and through the audience.)

(SIMONE *on a hike with her pupils. They carry packs. They climb and struggle forward toward the stage.)*

SIMONE: Let me carry that.

ONE: I can manage.

SIMONE: No, I'll carry your pack. The way is steep. *(To another)* Give me yours, too.

TWO: Thank you, Mademoiselle. I don't see how you do it—you don't look that strong. *(To audience member)* Would you pass my pack across to her? Thank you.

SIMONE: This is how one becomes strong.

THREE: How does one become in love?

SIMONE: Love?

FOUR: We understand what you teach us about physics. Could you tell us about love.

SIMONE: Love?

ALL: *(On stage now)* Falling in love. Loving. Being in love. Is it good or bad?

THREE: I want to know love.

SIMONE: Love?

ALL: Love!

SIMONE: Love is a serious thing.

ALL: Yes. Yes.

SIMONE: I have no advice to give you about love.

ALL: But you must—you know all about calculus.

SIMONE: Love? No, I have no advice to give you but I must warn you: love is a very serious thing.

ALL: *(Expectant)* Yes, Mademoiselle.

SIMONE: Love often means pledging one's own life and that of another human being forever. It always means that, unless one of the two treats the other as a plaything. In that case, a love is something odious. The essential point in love is this: one human being feels a vital need of another human being. The problem then arises of reconciling this need with freedom. A problem men have struggled with from time immemorial.

THREE: But if one is in love and pledged forever, why would you want to be free?

SIMONE: When I was your age, I was tempted to try to get to know love. I decided not to. I didn't want to commit my life in a direction impossible to foresee until I was sufficiently mature to know what I wish from life and what I expect from it.

FOUR: But I want to know now.

SIMONE: I'm not offering myself as an example; every life evolves by its own laws. But you might think about it. Love seems to me to involve an even more terrifying risk than blindly pledging one's own existence. I mean the risk, if one is the object of a profound love, of having absolute power over another human being. It's not that one should avoid love, but while you're very young, don't seek it, let it come and find you. Let's say hello to the mountains. There's new snow up there.

(They climb higher as SIMONE *walks back down mountain to her classroom. She finds several* SCHOOL BOARD MEMBERS *waiting for her.)*

HEAD OF BOARD: *(Holding four other* MEMBERS *in donkey reins)* Mademoiselle!

SIMONE: *(Walks in front of them reading a newspaper and puffing cigarette smoke like crazy)* M-m-m-m-m-m-m...

BOARD: Mademoiselle Instructor!

SIMONE: M-m-m-m-m-m-m-m... *(Continues to read and smoke).*

BOARD: The board finds that you are not paying attention to the board.

MEN: The board.

SIMONE: M-m-m-m-m-m-m-m...

BOARD: The board finds that you are not paying attention to the board.

MEN: Attention!

SIMONE: There is not enough time to pay attention to the students.

BOARD: You smoke.

MEN: Smoke!

SIMONE: Yes... *(Starts making note and takes out a cigarette).*

BOARD: You had the effrontery to print the students' work.

MEN: Work?

SIMONE: M-m-m-m-m-m-m-m...?

BOARD: This is nothing but the work of students. *(They shake printed papers in front of her.)*

MEN: Students!

SIMONE: It is the printed word.

BOARD: You were not authorized to print the work of nobodys.

MEN: Nobodys!

SIMONE: That is how they become somebodys.

BOARD: You are fired.

SIMONE: That is a fact I accepted in advance.

(The BOARD *exits in a chaos of entangled reins. Blackout)*

(SIMONE at a new school. It is a tougher school than before—the girls pretend to be blasé—no desks. They enter and stand around in what they think are tough, sophisticated poses.)

SIMONE: *Bonjour, Mesdemoiselles.*

CLASS: We don't want *bonjour.* We want life.

SIMONE: First you must learn to think.

CLASS: We want to live.

SIMONE: What is living?

CLASS: Enjoyment of the now.

SIMONE: If you cannot think, you will be robbed of the riches of the past and the future. To live in the now is pleasurable, but to think in the past and future is necessary to the development of your person and your family; therefore your roots and your country.

CLASS: Teach us to think.

SIMONE: It is hard, but if you pay attention, hard things can bring you good. Who would like to hike with me this weekend?

(Some hands up)

SIMONE: I have reports that there will be a break up of the ice, and possibly a flood. Who is strong enough to swim through the ice floes?

(Rest of hands up)

SIMONE: *Bon,* meet me at the river bank at three in the morning, with a little food for the two days, and matches wrapped carefully so that we can dry ourselves out, if we have to swim or rescue anyone. How many again wish to go on the hike?

(All hands up)

SIMONE: *Bon.* Girls are getting stronger. It's important. It's only through hard work that one understands one's intelligence.

GIRL: *(Delayed reaction)* Yeah.

(After much reluctance and teasing, they pull off their clothes and one by one dive into an ice river. One girl almost doesn't make it, but she is saved by another. They swim to high ground and put their clothes back on again. SIMONE *dresses and walks back to the classroom area.)*

(SIMONE walking and smoking in front of the SCHOOL BOARD*)*

BOARD: *Mademoiselle!*

SIMONE: M-m-m-m-m-m-m-m...

BOARD: *Mademoiselle,* you took the students on an unauthorized hike.

SIMONE: A swim...

BOARD: On an unauthorized swim under the most dangerous of conditions in the middle of winter.

SIMONE: The sun was out.

BOARD: There had been no permission granted by the school board or by the parents, and in fact you are to be considered under arrest for kidnapping.

SIMONE: *(Reading and walking and smoking)* M-m-m-m-m-m-m...

BOARD: Three people caught pneumonia.

SIMONE: Five were saved from drowning.

BOARD: Your students saved by other students.

SIMONE: An excellent experience in learning.

BOARD: You have been noticed to smoke and read and not pay attention at teachers' meetings.

SIMONE: M-m-m-m-m-m-m-m...

BOARD: You are hereby fired for insubordination, and endangering the lives and the moral attitudes of your pupils. You are hereby separated from us, uh fired, uh terminated.

SIMONE: *(Walking and smoking)* M-m-m-m-m-m-m-m... It is the condition of my teaching.

BOARD MEMBER: *(On way out)* And remove your coffee cup from the teachers' room. *(Exit)*

*(*SIMONE *meets with her old teacher and master* ALAIN.*)*

ALAIN: I've been following your articles closely.

SIMONE: They're only beginnings—I'm so awkward and confused.

ALAIN: No, I've never had a pupil like you. Your power of thought is rare.

SIMONE: All I have so far are hazy outlines and overweening ambitions.

ALAIN: Simone, on the contrary, it's like a game for you. I want to see you turn from playing games with abstract subtleties and train yourself in direct analysis.

SIMONE: I intend to. I'm going into the fields, I'm going into the factories, I'm going to study the relationship of the worker to his work. Modern science has lost its soul because it reasons only about conventional symbols—objects. They become objects by the fact that they are black marks on, white paper, but which are universal by virtue of their definition. There should be a new way of conceiving mathematics—a way that its theoretical and practical value would no longer be distinct, but would reside in analogies. In man's struggle with the universe, symbols would thus be relegated back to their rank as mere instruments, and their real function would be revealed, which is not to assist the understanding but the imagination. Scientific work would thus be seen to be in fact artistic work—namely, the training of the imagination. It would be necessary to foster and develop to the maximum the faculty of conceiving analogies without making use of algebraic symbols.

ALAIN: It sounds like an excellent project, but please Simone, when you write about it, try to make your language more penetrable to the ordinary mind.

SIMONE: I hope you'll excuse the confusion and disorder and also the audacity of my embryo ideas. If there is any value in them, it's clear that they could only be developed in silence. *(Hurriedly)* Also, I want to do a series of studies of the various existing forms of property, related to the idea that property consists, in reality, of the power to dispose of goods.

(Fade on ALAIN *as* SIMONE *walks into her room.)*

(1934. Several ex-pupils come to visit SIMONE *in the factory town where she works.)*

SIMONE: How good to see you again.

ONE: You didn't answer our letters.

TWO: We were worried.

THREE: Have you been ill?

SIMONE: Work in a factory isn't conducive to letter writing. How did you know where I was?

FOUR: The Derieu sisters.

SIMONE: Please don't tell anyone else. Promise me. This is the "contact with real life" we often talked about together.

ONE: But you're so frail.

SIMONE: Clumsy too, and slow, and not very robust.

TWO: How did they hire you?

ONE: There's no work these days.

SIMONE: One of my best friends knows the director of the company.

THREE: What's it like?

SIMONE: I'm glad to be working in a factory, but equally glad not to be compulsorily committed to it. It's simply a year's leave for "private study."

(As the speech continues, the ensemble enters and combines with one another to become the factory and machines. SIMONE *works at her machine, and the speed of her speech builds with the speed of her work.)*

SIMONE: If a man is very skilled, very intelligent, and very tough, there is just a chance, in the present conditions of French industry, for him to attain a factory job....

(Her visitors become machine parts.)

SIMONE: ...which offers interesting and humanly satisfying work: even so, these opportunities are becoming fewer every day, thanks to technical progress. But the women! The women are restricted to purely mechanical labor— Nothing is required of them but speed....

(The machines begin to work in earnest.)

SIMONE: When I say mechanical labor, don't imagine that it allows for daydreaming, much less reflection or thought. No. No. The tragedy is that, although the work is too mechanical to engage the mind, it prevents one from thinking of anything else. If you think, you work more slowly:

(The machines slow down and are silent.)

BARITONE: *(Sings)* Speed, speed, speed
Speed, speed, speed
Speed, or the sack
Speed, don't talk back
Speed, speed, speed
If you wish to feed.
(Speaks) Hurry up, Simone, you made only six hundred yesterday. If you make eight hundred today, maybe I won't fire you.

(The machines abruptly speed again.)

SIMONE: I still can't achieve the required speeds. I'm not familiar with the work, I'm innately awkward. I'm naturally slow moving, my head aches, and then I have the peculiar inveterate habit of thinking, which I can't shake off. Believe me, they would throw me out if I wasn't protected by influence. Theoretically, with the eight-hour day, one should have leisure, but really one's leisure hours are swallowed up by a fatigue which often amounts to a dazed stupor. Also, life in the factory involves a perpetual humiliating subordination, forever at the orders of foremen.

THREE: How can you stand the suffering?

SIMONE: I do suffer from it, but I'm more glad than I can say to be where I am. I've wanted it for I-don't-know-how-many years.

(The ensemble slowly breaks up the giant machine and exits, but SIMONE *continues to work as she speaks.)*

SIMONE: But I'm not sorry I didn't do it sooner, because it's at my age now that I can extract all the profit there is in the experience. Above all, I feel I've escaped from a world of abstractions to find myself among real men— some good and some bad, but with real goodness or badness. Goodness, especially when it exists in a factory, is something real. The least act of kindness, from a mere smile to some little service, calls for victory over fatigue and the obsession with pay—all the overwhelming influences which drive a man in on himself. Thought then calls for an almost miraculous effort of rising above the conditions of one's life. Because it's not like at a university, where one is paid to think, or pretend to think. In a factory one is paid not to think. So, if you ever recognize a gleam of intelligence, you can be sure it is genuine. Besides, I really find the machines themselves highly attractive and interesting.

(As members of ensemble arrive very slowly with real machines which they carry or manipulate, SIMONE *exits, as if in a trance. The ensemble members stare and work their machines as if the machines were controlling them. Slow fade.)*

(The old women pull the cord attached to one cherub. The belly opens and jewels made of jello and candy tumble out, showering the audience.)

END OF ACT ONE

ACT TWO

*(*SIMONE *enters with materials for letter. As she speaks the ensemble works out math forms [i.e. equations or symbols] with their bodies.)*

SIMONE: I need a physicist. I really need a physicist. Dearest Brother, please ask a physicist in America the following question: Planck justifies the introduction quanta of energy by the assimilation of entropy to a probability (Strictly, the logarithm of a probability): because, in order to calculate the probability of a macroscopic state of a system, it is necessary to postulate a finite number of corresponding microscopic states (Discrete states). So the justification is that the calculus of probabilities is numerical. But why was it not possible to use a continuous calculus of probabilities, with generalized numbers instead of discrete numbers (Considering that there are games of chance in which probability is continuous)? There would then have been no need of quanta. Why couldn't this have been tried? Planck says nothing about it. T does not know of a physicist here who could enlighten me. What do you think about this?

(The ensemble recites theories, goes into the audience to lecture them. Each actor should make up his own outrageous theories or speculations. The ensemble says to each other and the audience: "What do you think about this?" as they exit.)

SIMONE: Your reply about Planck did not satisfy me. Have you read St John of the Cross?

(Blackout. Ensemble stays in auditorium aisles, walking back and forth resolutely with eyes closed, whispering: "You don't interest me.")

SOPRANO: You don't interest me.

BARITONE: You don't interest me.

SOPRANO: I can't see you.

BARITONE: You can't see me.

SOPRANO: I look right through you. I look right through you because when I look, there is nothing there to see.

BARITONE: You don't interest me.
You don't interest me.
A Pharisee interests me more than how
Definitely
You don't interest me.

*(*SIMONE *on stage. This is her inside now: it slowly comes out as the singers sing, she passes people; as she passes them, she "fixes" on them. They feel it, and begin to reach out to her as if in a trance. They stop short of touching, but their eyes stay locked.)*

CHORUS: You have nothing for me.
I walk right through you
You don't even bore me
I've never heard you

SIMONE: *(Into mike)* No one can say you don't interest me, without showing grave cruelty and profound injustice to the uniqueness of the individual soul.

(The ensemble actors move up onto the stage and form moving human structures two and three people high.)

SIMONE: There is something sacred in every person.

CHORUS: There is something sacred in every person.

SIMONE: But it is not his person.

CHORUS: But it is not his person. Not his person? Not his person? But if not his person, then what is sacred in every person, if it is not his person?

SIMONE: It isn't his personality.

CHORUS: How can we sell him.

SIMONE: It isn't his personality, the personality he carries in his person.

CHORUS: But that's the package.

SIMONE: So much baggage.

CHORUS: Give me a good personality any day, and I can come with him in every way.

SIMONE: So much baggage.

SOPRANO: I agree with the chorus.

SIMONE: So much baggage.

BARITONE: I wouldn't mind for a while to carry the chorus for an extra mile.

SIMONE: Not his person, nor his thoughts
that I don't know.
Not his person, nor the way his arms grow.
Not his person, nor the way his eye is lit.
Not his person, but the total sacredness of
His presence. His presence that hurts us
when we must do without it.

CHORUS: His presence when we must do without King, Queen, father, father, mother, mother, sister, brother, friend, friend, friend, when you are gone and we have to live without your other.

SIMONE: Personality: Personality isn't what's sacred to me. Human personality means nothing to me. If it did, I could easily put out the eyes of anyone as Oedipus did his own. He still had exactly the same personality as before. I wouldn't have touched the person in him, I would only have destroyed his eyes. What is it? What is it that prevents me from putting out that man's eyes if I'm allowed to do it and if I feel like doing it?

CHORUS: Put out his eyes. Burn his thighs. Pull out his tongue. Put it in Washington where it belongs with the other rotting dungs of tongues.

(SIMONE addresses audience, while human pyramids made by the actors slowly revolve:)

SIMONE: The whole of your being is sacred to me, each one of you. But you are not sacred in all respects. You are not sacred because of your long bright hair, or your thick wrists, or your strong arms, or your kind heart, or the twinkle in your knowing eye, or even because your thoughts don't interfere with mine—none of these facts could keep me from hurting you without the knowledge that if I were to put out your eyes, your soul would be lacerated by knowing the pain, and the fact that *harm* was being done to you.

CHORUS: At the bottom of your heart
From the time you're a babe
Though you are miles apart
From your people...

DUET: You expect. You expect. You expect.

SOPRANO: With the certainty and the light
When the sperm entered the egg.

BARITONE: You expect to go on being remade
As the first
Ecstacy of the trinity
You were made.

(Pyramids disassemble and ensemble goes into dance formations.)

CHORUS: You were made You were made

SOPRANO: You were made in ecstacy

BARITONE: Lying down or standing up,

SOPRANO: Crossed horizons or against the G E

BARITONE: You were laid as you were made.

CHORUS: Ecstasy. Ecstasy. Ecstasy.

SIMONE: *(Tough and strong)* There is something in all of us that goes on indomitably expecting, in the teeth of all experience of crimes committed, suffered, and witnessed, that good....

CHORUS: *(Softly)* Good. Good.

SIMONE: That good and not evil will be done to you. It is this faith above all that is sacred in every human being.

ALL: Woo! *(Begin to dance)*

CHORUS: *(Like a thirties musical)* This above all
This above all,
This above all,
Learn to walk in higher heels
This above all, Baby
This above all
Learn to walk like you own
The world

(SIMONE exits.)

CHORUS: Learn how to kick and fly
Learn how to fly
Without getting sick
Learn how to throw away the stick
What you do is shove it up their ass
It's especially good
When they run out of gas
And you want nerve
To carry the verve
And show those nipples
Let them ripple
This above all
Get as tall as you can before
The geese begin
To step all over you and
When you fall
When you fall baby
Practice how to do it with a smile.
I'd walk a million miles
For one of your Luckies
My bucky little rag-time
Son-of-a-bitch
You witch
This was the days before Gary
Learned to switch his horse
And cocaine was running a close
Second to anyone's opium dream,

It's a scream
But this above all
This above all, learn how
To look like you're tall.
The fall is funnier.
The fall is funnier when you fall
Right off that wall
Oh be tall.
There might be a light
Outside the gate,
Don't you see it.
There might be a light
Outside the gate,
Don't you see it.
Let's burn gin to that.
We need a light to show
We're right,
We're right
Because we know in the
Bottoms of your cups
That might can't conquer right,
That might can't conquer right, etc.
(Softer under next two lines)

BARITONE: There is no war on.
There is no war on.

(Blackout)

(Series of rapid scenes:)

(Out of work men of the town are pounding huge stones with sledgehammers.)

SIMONE: Why are you cracking the rocks?

ONE: We have to.

SIMONE: Are you going to build a wall or a garden?

TWO: We're out of work.

SIMONE: What do you mean you're out of work, you're working harder than I do.

THREE: We have to do this or they won't give us unemployment checks.

SIMONE: Give me one of those and I'll help you.

(She stands beside the men and though she's slower, still works. Then all run to the next scene.)

(In the factory. The workers are having a sit-in. They sit on the floor, arms linked and swaying, singing "The International." SIMONE *is there too, arms linked with*

the workers, between two men. Two men in charge of running the factory are conferring with one another as the song ends. They turn and shout at the workers.)

MANAGER ONE: Seven percent increase.

WORKERS: Fifteen.

MANAGER TWO: Seven percent.

WORKERS: Fifteen.

(They yell this back and forth in mounting crescendo. Moment of silence)

WORKERS: Fifteen and a joint committee of workers and management.

MANAGER ONE: I'll hire and fire whom I choose.

WORKERS: Joint committee or no work done. Joint committee or no work done.

MANAGER TWO: We'll close down the factory.

MANAGER ONE: We'll close down the factory—that will put some sense into you.

WORKERS: Good, good, good. Close down the factory and we'll take it over and run it ourselves. We run this factory ourselves anyway.

MANAGER ONE: This is a gross infringement of liberty.

WORKERS: We want fifteen percent more.

MANAGER TWO: You make me sick.

WORKERS: Fifteen! Fifteen! Fifteen! Fifteen! Fifteen! We'll make you sick, all right. *(Go for the managers' throats—then immediately transform into Comrades at a meeting.)*

(A political meeting of leftist coalition parties.)

SIMONE: *(Addressing the crowd)* Friends and workers. Some of us have been greatly troubled and alarmed by news of the continuing purge in Russia. I'm afraid that in this struggle that begins to look like the classic struggle between the conservatives and the innovators the value of life is being forgotten. The conservatives do not know what to conserve, and the innovators do not know what to innovate—

VOICE: Revisionists! Traitorous revisionists!

SIMONE: Please, I ask you to pay one more minute of attention. It's true so far as we know it that Stalin's lieutenant S M Kirov was murdered. But Stalin is using this crime as a tool against many comrades who fought and sacrificed many long years to bring Marxist–Leninist concepts into being. If he is allowed to continue unchecked in this "purge," there will be no chance for the dictatorship of the proletariat, because all his brothers will have been eliminated resulting in the dictatorship of one man, Joseph Stalin. We must show him that there is a world of opinion, considered and humane opinion by his brothers in other countries that condemn his actions, that he must cease and desist in this cruel persecution—

ONE: Traitor! She's a Trotskyite.

(Some people walk out.)

TWO: The purge is just and moral. Those men were working with the Germans to overthrow Stalin and so are you. I denounce Simone as a Trotskyite!

THREE: Get her.

FOUR: Beat her up.

(They move slowly toward her.)

FIVE: Smash her mouth.

SIX: Don't let her open it again.

SEVEN: Kill her.

SIMONE: I'm not a Trotskyite, I belong to no party. I am against totalitarianism in all its forms. If this "purge" continues in Russia, Stalin will succeed in creating a monolithic totalitarian unity and it will be an end to Lenin's ideals and an end to people's democracy.

EIGHT: Get her. Trotskyite!

(They grab her. NINE *and a small group of friends holding two guns surround* SIMONE *to protect her.)*

TEN: I support Stalin.

ELEVEN: Shut that Trotskyite's trap.

SIMONE: I'm not a Trotskyite, I'm a Frenchman.

NINE: Simone, comrade, stay in the middle of us. We'll get you out safely.

TWELVE: You're a Trotskyite and you're a Jew!

(With some brief scuffling, they get her out of the meeting.)

(Outside the meeting, SIMONE *is talking with man who rescued her.)*

SIMONE: Thank you, Pierre. I'll never forget your kindness and your bravery.

PIERRE: Those Communist fanatics want to drive us into war. You know that during the general strike they were working on the side of management to prevent our strike!

SIMONE: I know, because they want all the armaments built as soon as possible to speed up the prospect of war. Well, I'm going off to fight in a war, a just war. I've decided to go to Spain. At least there, my one pair of hands might be useful.

PIERRE: Be careful your rifle doesn't backfire on you, you're not so clever with your hands.

SIMONE: Don't worry. I'm a pacifist. I'll never carry a rifle, there's other work to do.

(Blackout)

*(*SIMONE *in Spain: on the banks of the Ebro River. The Anarchist forces she has joined are on one side and Fascist forces are on the other. Sound of airplane overhead.)*

CAPTAIN: Get that plane!

(The squadron, including SIMONE, *who does have a rifle in hand, begin to shoot.* SIMONE *lies on her back and shoots straight up into the air.)*

CAPTAIN: The pisser's flying too high.

(Sound of small bomb exploding)

CAPTAIN: Their bombs are getting smaller. That means we're winning.

(A squad of men come in dragging two priests.)

ONE: Captain! Captain! Look what we found hiding in the rushes on the river bank.

CAPTAIN: This will make forty priests we've shot. *(He points at one of them.)* Kneel with your head in prayer.

(The other men laugh; SIMONE *lowers her rifle. The* CAPTAIN *shoots the priest. He falls forward and dies, crying out "Jesus" in Spanish.)*

CAPTAIN: *(To the second priest)* We're going to let you go, so you can tell the rest of your brothers to get the hell out of our country. Get going, on the double.

(As the priest turns, he shoots him too. The men laugh again. SIMONE *throws down her rifle.)*

CAPTAIN: Squadron. Attention! We're going out on patrol. The Fascists are just across the river, and at dawn we'll start picking them off. Simone?

SIMONE: I'll stay in camp and cook.

TWO: *(Sotto voce, to a comrade)* Thank God, she awkward with a gun, she'll kill one of us one day.

CAPTAIN: Good, you stay and fry me those chickens we commandeered. I haven't had meat in two months.

(They march off stealthily. SIMONE *puts a pot of oil on the fire. Another woman helps her peel vegetables to throw into the oil. They pluck chickens.)*

SIMONE: Atrocities. On both sides.

WOMAN: *(Laughing)* Did you see how the other thought God had saved his life?

SIMONE: How can you laugh at a thing like that?

WOMAN: It was funny. Did you see the look on his face after the bullet hit his head?

SIMONE: This isn't our war. This is nothing but a war fought by Germany against Russia. We're fools and pawns. *(She's so angry she hits the pot of oil so hard that it spills over onto her leg. She screams and falls.)*

WOMAN: Oh, my God, your leg is burning. *(She runs out screaming for help.)*

*(*SIMONE *alone in a field hospital reciting math formulas to avoid the pain. Her* FATHER *and* MOTHER *rush on.)*

FATHER: Simone, my precious.

MOTHER: Simone, my own.

FATHER: It's taken us a month to find you.

MOTHER: *(Not daring to look)* How bad?

FATHER: What butcher is tending you? This dressing hasn't been changed in a week, half the flesh is exposed. *(He brings things out of his bag, gives her a sedative.)* Here, this will still the pain.

SIMONE: I'm getting used to it.

MOTHER: We'll take her home to recover.

SIMONE: No, no, father, I have to rejoin my unit.

FATHER: I'm your father and your doctor and you'll do as I say. Let's get a stretcher.

*(*MOTHER *and* FATHER *exit.)*

*(*SIMONE *is alone in her room. Visitation)*

SIMONE: My spirit is sick. Do I have a spirit. Pain in the throat, double pain. I can't swallow but I feel constantly that I'll vomit. My spine. My spine is sick. I can't work and that makes me sicker. Not to be able to work. No work. Work beating in my head, but my hands refuse to close around a pencil. My mind won't work for me, but something in me is working, and I'm so sick and weak. The struggle against this stupid body is getting too much to bear. I've got to think my way out of it but I can't think. My God, my God, I can't think. I can't move out of this bed. My God I can't stand. I can't walk. I can't think, I can't think, this stupid pain. My God. My God, I need something. I need something. I need my work. I need to work. Any work. I'd cry for joy to be able to bend in the dirt and pick up potatoes till my back ached from work. Honest work. Not the work of fighting this endless headache. I'll try to vomit. I'll get it out, I'll vomit out the pain. Oh my God, can't I get any light into my head? My God! MyGod! MyGod!

(The entire cast comes on stage and lifts SIMONE *up, giving her a total caress. They hum. They take her pain into their bodies, until all but five who lift her up to God are feeling the pain that she had. As they lift* SIMONE, *they take her clothes off and as the clothes fall, other actors put them on, continuing a pain centered at a point in the body the garment covers. They lift her straight up if they can, her arms outstretched, smiling with her eyes closed. They put her down and exit.)*

LOVE III
The Poem of George Herbert

SIMONE: *(Transfixed, warmed, and filled with divine love, sings)*:
Love bade me welcome
Yet my soul drew back,
Guiltie of dust and sinne.
But quick-eye'd love,
Observing me grow slack
From my first entrance in,
Drew nearer to me,
Sweetly questioning,
If I lack'd any thing.

A guest, I answer'd
Worthy to be here:
Love said, you shall be he.
I the unkinde, ungratefull?
Ah my deare,
I cannot look on thee.
Love took my hand,
And smiling did reply
Who made the eyes but I?

Truth Lord, but I have marr'd them
Let my shame go where
It doth deserve.
And know you not, sayes love,
Who bore the blame?
My deare, then I will serve.
You must sit down, sayes love,
And taste my meat:
So I did sit and eat

(Ensemble dancers enter and dance with SIMONE, *while the chorus sings:* Song for Simone, *opera singers, chorus and dancers.)*

CHORUS: I believe God created
So he could be loved

God created
So that he, God could be loved

But God can't create God
God can't create anything to be God

But God cannot be loved by anything
Which isn't God, God needs
God to sing
God needs God to sing to him of his love
Of God for God
God needs God to love him into God.

This is a contradiction!
Not a fiction but a perfect
A perfect, an exact, contradiction.
I have the conviction
That this contradiction
Contains in itself necessity itself.
This is not perversity
Or play of mind
But this is a perfect contradiction.
Contradiction creates action
This is a contradiction that defines
Necessity. Necessity. *Necessity!*

But every contradiction
Has the condition of resolving
Itself through the process
Through the process of
Becoming, becoming, becoming,
Becoming, *Becoming!*
God created me to see the sea
And to love him
"I"—"I"—"I" this finite being
I this this "I"
"I" and "I," this little "I"
I can't love God
Until
Until, through the action of grace
That takes over the empty space
Of my total soul—
The grace that fills my soul
The grace to make me whole with God.

And as this little "I" disappears
God loves himself
God loves himself

By my giving up my "I"
As I become not "I"
As I cannot see the sky, nor be the sky
God loves me as I disappear

I give God to God and
And God loves himself
As this process goes on forever
Therefore God
Has created time
Time is indifferent to me,
There is all the time
In my short world
For me to become not me

So that God
So that God can love himself
This
This
This
This
This
This is the necessity, the necessity, the necessity
Necessity!

(A police station, three policemen and a secretary)

ONE: It's been reported that you are a Gaulliste.

TWO: You were seen distributing *Témoignage chrétien.*

THREE: An illegal paper.

SIMONE: But a higher literary style than the government censors.

TWO: So you admit to this underground activity.

SIMONE: I admit I read everything I can get my hands on.

ONE: If you don't tell us who the rest of your comrades are...

TWO: You'll go to prison.

THREE: And I'll personally see that you, a teacher of philosophy, will be put into the same cells as the prostitutes.

ONE: As the prostitutes.

SIMONE: I've always wanted to know about such circles of women. It will be a very good opportunity to get to know them. Yes, please do send me to jail.

TWO: She's crazy.

THREE: She's crazy, no professor of philosophy would want to associate with filthy prostitutes.

SIMONE: But I would. It's a subject I haven't had time to study yet.

ONE: Release the prisoner. She's crazy.

(Blackout)

*(*SIMONE *arrives in Marseilles and goes to the Dominican monastery where she can ask a priest who is helping people to get out of the country for work while she waits to get out too. There are several people before her, one is just leaving.)*

MAN: Thank you for the passport, Father. You've saved my life.

FATHER: *(A warm man with natural charm)* Safe journey and God bless, my son.

SIMONE: *(Enters shyly)* Excuse me, Father. I hate to take away from your valuable time, but I need some sort of work, preferably manual labor, where I can fade into a group. Is there any farm work about, perhaps the grape harvest?

FATHER: My child, you look so frail, I hardly...

SIMONE: I'm not as frail as I look—I've worked in factories.

FATHER: You don't speak like a factory worker.

SIMONE: You know about the laws: we're not allowed to work. My family and I are bound for Morocco on our way to the States. I want work to occupy my time.

FATHER: Are you sure you can manage. The sun's hot.

SIMONE: Good.

FATHER: I have a friend, just outside of town who might take you on....

SIMONE: Thank you Father...Father...may I come to speak with you sometime again...

FATHER: I'm taken up with many duties besides my clerical ones—so many people are being hounded down by the police, so many people need help and advice.

SIMONE: I'd like to speak to you about Christ.

(They freeze, walk in a circle. She hesitantly approaches him again.)

SIMONE: After working in the factories, I finally understood affliction. I began to see myself as a slave and I was often able to rise above the physical affliction of my headaches. Then in a Chapel in Solesmes where I'd gone to hear the Gregorian music at Easter I was able to listen to the music in spite of pain. By an extreme effort of attention I was able to get outside this miserable flesh, leaving it to suffer by itself, and I found a pure and perfect joy in the unspeakable beauty of the chanting and the words. During the time I was there I also met a young man, a messenger I think of him now, who introduced me to George Herbert's poem "Love." From then on whenever my headache would reach a painful crisis, I would recite this poem fixing all my attention on it, clinging with all my soul to the tenderness it enshrines. One day, while saying this poem with all my attention, Christ Himself came down and He took possession of me.

FATHER: Did you see Him?

SIMONE: No, it was the presence of love, of infinite love, a certainty of love, a love which I have never sought and which I'd never thought existed.

FATHER: My child, are you seeking Catholic instruction?

SIMONE: I don't wish Baptism.

FATHER: But that is complete union.

SIMONE: I prefer to stand at the door of the church.

FATHER: Then you're still a long way from Christianity.

(Again they freeze, walk in a small circle, relax, and she approaches him again.)

SIMONE: Every day before I go out to harvest I say the "Our Father" in Greek. I try to do this with the utmost attention and if I do, Christ comes nearer to me now than He did that first time.

FATHER: It gives me joy to see the light growing within you.

(They freeze, she kneels and says the Pater Noster in Greek, or any language the actress would like. Then she stands. They approach each other again.)

FATHER: My child, you suffer too much from your former intellectual life. You're confusing reality with distortions of it. I feel you're hardest and most severe in your judgments on that which could touch you the most.

SIMONE: I have to beware of you. Friendship and the power of suggestion is what I'm most susceptible to.

FATHER: But Baptism is—

SIMONE: I don't want to belong to any groups. I want to be invisible, so that I can move among all groups. I'm suspicious of structures, and especially the structure of the Catholic Church, it has been totalitarian since the time of the Roman Empire.

FATHER: You're still locked into the narrow philosophy of Spinoza.

SIMONE: I'd never read any of the mystics till my love of Christ, but now I see that Dionysus and Osiris are an early form of Christ. The *Bhagavad-Gita* when read aloud is a marvelous Christian sound. Yes, even Plato was a mystic. I see the *Iliad* now as bathed in Christian light.

FATHER: Your early intellectual training and culture are keeping you from contemplating the true mysteries of the Church dogma. Baptism is a complete union.

SIMONE: I want to thank you for bearing with me for so long. I'd never really considered the problem of Baptism as a practical one before. I'm sorry to withhold from you what would give you the greatest joy, but God has other uses for me. If I felt His command to be baptized, I would come running at once. For now I think God doesn't want me in the Church, perhaps at the moment of death...

FATHER: It's my only concern that you stay in readiness....

SIMONE: I could only say all this to you because I'm leaving tomorrow. Goodbye, you've been a father and a brother to me.... It's impossible to think of you without thinking of God. *(Exit)*

(Outside a Harlem church. Sounds of gospel music.)

CLAIRE: We're the only white people here. Are you sure we won't offend?

SIMONE: I've been to a different church in Harlem every Sunday since I arrived in New York.

CLAIRE: I'm a bit uneasy.

SIMONE: Are you my friend?

CLAIRE: Yes, you know it; we've talked for days and nights together.

SIMONE: Will you be my friend?

CLAIRE: We're going to get back to France together; we're going to sabotage the Nazis together.

SIMONE: Come, let's enter this church of God.

*(*CLAIRE *presses* SIMONE*'s hand and they enter the church together. A song is ending as they sit in first row of auditorium.)*

PREACHER: Brothers and Sisters, let us pray for our President. Let us pray for our great President Franklin Delano Roosevelt. He faces trying times in this terrible war. The people on the East is attacking us, and the people in the West is attacking us. Brothers and Sisters, let us pray to Jesus to help our President in these terrible times so that with the help of You, oh Lord, and Your chosen Son, Jesus, our President Roosevelt can make peace all over God's great, green and beautiful garden.

Give yourself up to the power of Our Lord,
Give yourself up to the power of Our Lord,
If you ever gonna find yourself
You got to give yourself up,
Give yourself up to the power of Our Lord.

PREACHER: *(Sings)* Brothers and sisters
Brothers and sisters
What sex is Jesus?
What sex is God?

CHORUS: *(Repeats and claps)* What sex is Jesus?
What sex is God?

PREACHER: What sex was Mary?
What sex was Saul
After he changed his name to Paul?
Jesus lets us into him
Both men and women
Jesus lets us into him
Both saints and sinnin'

MALE SINGER: Simone, Simone, Simone. Your body is woman and your head talks to God.

(Brings SIMONE *on stage.)*

CHORUS: Jesus had a prick
He didn't use to fuck with
But penetrating the waters
He made enough fishes to
Feed the multitude
Without licking essential oils, Jesus
Made bread without an oven
He fed a thousand dozens

CLAIRE: Simone, I feel I have to leave. I'm overcome with emotion, I feel I might dissolve. Let's go before I can't control myself any longer.

SIMONE: Get up with the congregation. Let's go with them to Jesus.

CLAIRE: I'm afraid.

SIMONE: You're ready to face the Nazis, but you're still not ready to approach God?

(They rise and join the congregation, who are singing and jitterbugging and throwing themselves into a trance with their closeness to the Lord. A woman leaps up from the congregation. She is possessed and sings. The chorus echoes her.)

WOMAN: Oh Lord, oh Lord, oh Lord
I'm opening up for you
Oh Lord, oh Lord
I'm ready to receive
My Jesus,
Oh Jesus, son of God,
I'll do right to you

My arms are open
My arms are open
Oh Lord, oh Jesus,
I'll give it all back to you.

Take my hands
Take my feet

(Repeat all the parts of the body till end of scene.)

CHORUS: She's a Jesus lady
She's a Jesus lady
What sex is Jesus?
Jesus done entered her
Jesus done entered her
Jesus done entered her

PREACHER: She's a Jesus lady
She's a Jesus lady
She's a Jesus lady
Right now and forevermore.
(Exit)

(French headquarters in England)

(As this scene progresses it should be as if SIMONE *is visiting a series of offices. Each official, and, if possible, his secretary too, gets taller and fatter, until the final one is a giant figure somewhat like De Gaulle. On screens and slides, on scrolls, that come down, from projections, etc., we should see films and stills of people in their death agonies.)*

SIMONE: *Bonjour, mon cher ami.* It's good to see you again. I had no idea how long it would take me to get to London.

MAN: Did you go to America?

SIMONE: Only because I thought it would be a faster way to get here, so that I can be of service to France. It took much longer than I'd hoped.

MAN: Your parents?

SIMONE: They wanted to escape from the anti-Semitism without being separated from me. I've come to offer you my services to work for France. I distributed one of the most important clandestine publications in the free zone, *Les Cahiers du témoignage chrétien.* But when I was there, I was consoled by sharing the suffering of my country. I've come back to offer my self, because France's misfortunes hurt me much more at a distance than when I was there. Leaving was like tearing up my roots. But I only left in the hope that I could take a bigger and more effective part in the efforts, dangers and sufferings of this great struggle. I have an idea.

MAN: Perhaps you'd like to explain it to the Captain?

CAPTAIN: *(Enters and bows) Mademoiselle.*

SIMONE: I have an idea.

CAPTAIN: *Bon,* they are needed.

SIMONE: This idea will save the lives of many soldiers.

CAPTAIN: *Bon.*

SIMONE: Many needless deaths happen on the field due to the lack of immediate care, cases of shock, exposure, loss of blood.

CAPTAIN: Correct.

SIMONE: Please consider it seriously, I want to work in secret operations, preferably dangerous.

CAPTAIN: Perhaps you should speak to the major. *(Exits)*

MAJOR: *(Enters) Mademoiselle.*

SIMONE: I really believe I can be useful. I appeal to you as a comrade to get me out of this painful moral situation. A lot of people don't understand why it's a painful moral situation, but you certainly do. We had a great deal in common when we were students together. It gave me a real joy to learn that you have such an important position in London. I'm relying on you.

MAJOR: We can certainly use your brilliant mind. You were first in your class.

SIMONE: I want action. Here's the idea: create a special body of front line nurses.

MAJOR: Of women?

SIMONE: *(Nods and hurries on)* It would be a very mobile organization and should always be at the points of greatest danger.

MAJOR: But the horrors of war at the front—

SIMONE: —are so distinct today in everyone's imagination that one can regard any woman who is capable of volunteering for such work as being very probably capable of performing it.

MAJOR: But they risk certain death.

SIMONE: They would need to have a good deal of courage. They would need to offer their lives as a sacrifice.

MAJOR: But we have never put our women in such danger. That's why we men leave for the front to defend our homes and families.

SIMONE: There is no reason to regard the life of a woman, especially if she has passed her first youth without marrying or having children, as more valuable than a man's life All the less so if she has accepted the risk of death.

MAJOR: But how to regulate...

SIMONE: Simply make mothers, wives and girls below a certain age ineligible.

MAJOR: I'm considering the idea.

SIMONE: The moral support would be inestimable. They would comfort the men's last moments, they would mitigate by their presence and their words the agony of waiting for the arrival of the stretcher-bearers. You must understand the essential role played in the present war by moral factors. They count for very much more than in past wars. It's one of the main reasons for Hitler's successes that he was the first to see this.

MAJOR: I believe you should explain this to the General. *(Exits)*

(GENERAL enters, only nods.)

SIMONE: *(Exhorting)* Hitler has never lost sight of the essential need to strike everybody's imagination; his own people's, his enemies', and the innumerable spectators. One of his most effective instruments has been the S S. These men are unmoved by suffering and death, either for themselves or for all the rest of humanity. Their heroism originates from an extreme brutality that corresponds perfectly to the spirit of the regime and the designs of their leader. We cannot copy these methods of Hitler's. First, because we fight in a different spirit and with different motives. But when it is a question of striking the imagination, copies never succeed. Only the new is striking. We give a lot of thought to propaganda for the rear, yet it is just as important at the front. At the rear, propaganda is carried on by words. At the front, verbal propaganda must be replaced by the propaganda of action.

GENERAL: What do you propose?

SIMONE: A simple corps of women performing a few humane services in the very center of the battle—the climax of inhumanity—would be a signal of defiance of the inhumanity which the enemy has chosen for himself and which he also compels us to practice. A small group of women exerting day after day a courage of this kind with a maternal solicitude would be a spectacle so new, so much more striking than Hitler's young S S fanatics. The contrast between these women and the S S would make a more telling argument than any propaganda slogan. It would illustrate with supreme clarity the two roads between which humanity today is forced to choose.

GENERAL: *Merci.* A very good idea. We will think about it. In the meantime we have some essential work for you to do.

(Typewriter and mounds of papers are wheeled out.)

GENERAL: Four copies of each as soon as possible. There's a war on.

(Blackout. The old men pull the cord attached to their cherub and ashes, bones and plastic baby dolls shower the audience.)

(SIMONE, with a mike on a high platform, addresses a crowd. As she speaks, lights begin to go off and on. Strange noises—gunshot. Bit by bit the people leave and take up sides to fight the war.)

SIMONE: We're in a conflict with no definable objective.When there is no objective, there is no common measure of proportion. Compromise is inconceivable. The only way the importance of such a battle can be measured is by the sacrifices it demands. From this it follows that the sacrifices already made are a perpetual argument for new sacrifices. There would never be any reason to stop killing and dying, except that there is fortunately a limit to human endurance. *(Silence)* This paradox is so extreme as to defy analysis. And yet the most perfect example of it is known to every so called educated man, but, by a sort of taboo, we read it without understanding. The Greeks and Trojans massacred one another for ten years on account of Helen. Not one of them except the dilettante warrior Paris cared two straws about her. All of them wished she'd never been born. Its importance was simply imagined as corresponding to the deaths incurred and the further massacres expected.

(Lights flicker and go out. People crawl in aisles and over audience. Lights—flashing; crying, running.)

SIMONE: This implied an importance beyond all reckoning. Hector foresaw that his city would be destroyed, his father and brothers massacred, his wife degraded to a slavery worse than death. Achilles knew that he was condemning his father to the miseries and humiliations of a defenseless old age. All of them were aware that their long absence at the war would bring ruin on their homes; yet no one felt the cost too great, because they were all in pursuit of a literal non-entity whose only value was in the price paid for it!

(Silence—then the war begins again.)

SIMONE: For the clear-sighted, there is no more distressing symptom of this truth than the unreal character of most of the conflicts that are taking place today. They have even less reality than the war between Greeks and Trojans. At the heart of the Trojan War there was at least a woman, and what is more, a woman of perfect beauty. For our contemporaries the role of Helen is played by words with capital letters. If we grasp one of these words, all swollen with blood and tears, and squeeze it, we find it is empty.

(Silence—then just breathing. Then war begins again.)

SIMONE: Words with content and meaning are not murderous. When empty words are given capital letters, then men on the slightest pretext will begin shedding blood. In these conditions the only definition of success is to crush a rival group of men who have a hostile word on their banners. When a word is properly defined, it loses its capital letter and can no longer serve either as a banner or as a hostile slogan.

(Screams. Someone is shot while pleading not to be. Silence)

SIMONE: It becomes simply a sign, helping us to grasp some concrete reality, concrete objective or method of activity. To clarify thought, to discredit the intrinsically meaningless words and to define the use of others by precise analysis—to do this, strange though it may appear, might be a way of saving human lives.

BARITONE: How like a woman to reduce war to semantics.

SOPRANO: How like a man to reduce war to mathematics.

(All the men are lying on stage or in aisles. The women drag their bodies to a pile on stage as SIMONE *speaks.)*

SIMONE: My dearest brothers, lying twenty years in your hospital beds, you are privileged men. The present state of the world is reality for you. You are experiencing more reality in your constant affliction than those who are dying in the war, at this moment killing and dying, wounded and being wounded. Because they are taken unaware. They don't know where they are. They don't know what is happening to them. People not in the middle of the war don't know what's real. But you men have been repeating in thought, for twenty years, that act which took and then released so many men. But you were seized permanently. And now the war is here again to kill millions of men. You are ready to think. Or if you are still not quite ready—as I feel you are not—you only have the thinnest shell to break before emerging from the darkness inside the egg into the light of truth. It is a very ancient image. The egg is this world we see. The bird in it is Love, the Love which is God Himself and which lives in the depths of every man, though at first as an invisible seed.

MAN: Will you help me kill myself.

SIMONE: Break your shell and you will no longer be inside. Space is opened and torn apart.

(Silence for a moment. In pain and twitching like the men, SIMONE*'s voice at first mirrors migraine pain, but then rises above the pain through the speech.)*

SIMONE: The spirit throws the miserable body in some corner and is transported to a point outside space. Space has become an infinity. The moment stands still.

WOMEN: *(Singing, facing audience from stage or in position in aisles)*
The moment stands still!
The moment stands still!
The moment stands still!
The moment stands still!
The moment stands still!
The silence is dense.
Sounds
Sounds
Silence is.
The whole of space is filled
Not an absence of sound

But the moment is filled
With the secret word.
Once you break out of your shell
You will know what is real
About war.
You will know the secret word
You never knew before,
Not the absence of sound
But love, love, love, love, love.

SIMONE: *(Speaking)* It is not an absence of sound, but a positive object of sensation. *(Singing)*
You, when you've emerged
From the shell
Will know the reality of war.
The most precious reality to know
Is that, war is unreality itself.

*(Speaking)*You are infinitely privileged. War has permanently lodged in your body.

WOMEN: *(Singing)* War is affliction,
Fortunate are you to know

SIMONE: War is affliction. It isn't easy to direct one's thoughts toward affliction voluntarily. To think affliction, it's necessary to bear it in one's flesh, driven very far in like a nail, and for a long time, so that thought may have time to grow strong enough to regard it.

WOMEN: *(Singing)* War is affliction,
Fortunate are we to know.
Fortunate are we.
War is affliction.
Fortunately we cannot see it.
War is affliction.

SIMONE: You have the opportunity and the function of knowing the truth of the world's affliction. Contemplate its reality!

(Men rise and take their places facing the audience.)

(SIMONE *begins to move through them, climbing ever higher on the platforms.)*

MAN ONE: Eat, Simone.

(She shakes her head and moves up ramp.)

MAN TWO: Eat, Simone.

(She shakes head and climbs to highest platform. She's weak and must hold onto the bars to stand up. A woman mounts an auditorium platform and mechanically intones.)

WOMAN DOCTOR: *(At an inquest, British accent)* I tried to persuade Simone to take some food, and she said she would try. She did not eat, however, and gave as a reason the thought of her people in France starving.

ENSEMBLE: *(Whispers over and over)* Strange suicide.

WOMAN DOCTOR: She died on the twenty-fourth of August, and death was due to cardiac failure due to degeneration through starvation.

BARITONE: *(Singing, as a judge)* Simone, aged thirty-four, committed suicide by starvation while the balance of her mind was disturbed.

(CHORUS speaks)

WOMEN: Strange suicide. Strange suicide.

MEN: Refused to eat.

WOMEN: Strange suicide. Strange suicide.

MEN: Refused to eat.

MEN & WOMEN: *(As lights begin to dim on ensemble)* She refused. She refused. She refused.

WOMAN ONE: She wouldn't eat. She wouldn't eat the bombs of the Germans, she wouldn't eat the furnaces of the Nazis. She swallowed the pride of France, but it didn't stick to her ribs.

CHORUS: Strange, strange, strange, strange, strange—
Simone wouldn't eat.
Simone wouldn't eat.

WOMAN TWO: Her soul was full, she didn't have to eat. There's no such thing as a personality. There's no such thing as a mind when the body dies. The mind can die before the body dies.

WOMAN THREE: She wouldn't eat. She wouldn't eat. She couldn't eat when others starved. She wouldn't eat while Hitler carved the meat of her countryside.

WOMAN FOUR: While everyone else lived on spoiled cabbage leaves and boiled rainwater, Simone ate nothing.

(Blackout on ensemble)

WOMAN FIVE: How thin she must have been. What a tiny coffin they must have buried her in.

(Pin spot on SIMONE, dimming slowly, slowly, slowly, slowly to black.)

END OF PLAY

BABES IN THE BIGHOUSE

Book and Lyrics by Megan Terry
Structure by Jo Ann Schmidman
Music by John J Sheehan

dedicated to the women and men in prison in the U S and
Canada who asked us to make this play
and to John J Sheehan, Composer, Conductor, Performer

BABES IN THE BIGHOUSE (A Documentary Fantasy About Life in a Women's Prison) was first presented at the Omaha Magic Theatre, Omaha, Nebraska, on 15 November 1974. It then toured the U S, in O M T's repertory for the next three years. The following appeared in BABES at various times:

Jill Anderson
Carol Dietz
Joe Guinan
Judith Katz
Jim Laferla
James Larson
Nancy Larson
Michael Malstead
Jo Ann Schmidman
Rae Ann Schmitz
Elisa Stacy
Mary Thatcher
Stephanie Toothacher
Kate Ullman
Donna Young

Director .... JoAnn Schmidman
Score composed and played by .... John J Sheehan
Song: Pardon Me *composed by* .... Jill Anderson
Set design .... Megan Terry & JoAnn Schmidman
Light design .... Judy Gillespie & Colbert McClellan
Net design one .... Mitza Thompson
Net design two .... Diane Degan

ENVIRONMENT

For the Omaha Magic Theatre production the playing area was a rectangular shape ten feet by forty feet. This was dictated by the shape of our building. There were two to three rows of raised seating for the audience along the forty foot sides. Double-decker cells for the inmates were constructed of metal scaffolding (which we painted bright yellows, reds, blues and greens) at one end of the playing area. At the O M T the cells were at the entrance to the theater. The audience, upon entering and buying tickets, were immediately confronted with the cells, each individually outlined with seven-watt Christmas tree lights. The small corridor leading to the seating area was roped off so that the audience was confined in the lobby.

While the audience waits, an audiotape plays. We made our tape by going door-to-door and asking people on the street questions about what they think goes on inside a women's prison. We found that the majority of responses were influenced by the gross amount of cheap sex novels, "grade C" drive-in movies and personal fantasies, all having to do with women locked up, as punishment, together. Therefore, the actors at O M T were dressed in various combinations of corsets, long gloves, feathers and furs, garters, fishnet hose, spike heels and too much makeup.

Opposite the cells at the other end of the playing area is a six-inch-high platform (five feet by six feet). A net hangs from the ceiling grazing the length of the platform. The net at O M T was made from an old volleyball net. Affixed to the net were crocheted aprons, doilies and other articles which the prisoners made in crafts class. There is a 3' opening slit in the center of the net.

At various times in the play, the platform is used as the warden's office, the doctor's office and solitary confinement ("The Hole").

The area between the platform and the cells represents at various times—hallways, the shower room, the yard and the sewing room. The dominant dramatic image in the play is "how the women walk." They walk the halls from cells to laundry to cafeteria, etc.

As the actors/inmates walk through the hall, they focus their attention on the rhythms inside their heads.

The interior rhythms should be projected outward in the way each individual walks. Each actor selects many characters to play throughout the evening and this will be evident in the transformation of the walks.

NOTE: Reasons for "the interior" are to maintain sanity, to withdraw from others, to space out, to state who they are, etc, or to show dominance or confusion as a guard. When actors aren't involved in a scene with dialogue, at the director's discretion they may continue the "walks."

The other dominant dramatic image in the play is the "imposing of wills." Inmates impose wills on one another and on the guards. Several weeks of workshop were spent working on "the wills." We discovered when one imposed her will on another, the object of the will imposition resisted. This created tension—a push/pull situation—and the image was momentarily frozen until a guard came upon them, an inmate approached or a prison noise would startle them. (These may be actual or imagined.) This caused those involved in the imposing of wills to pull away, change their focus, break the tension and thus change the image, returning to "the walks." O M T never performs BABES in proscenium. When we tour to a proscenium theater, we have all the audience seated on stage, in rows of seats facing each other along the longest side of the stage (on a deep, narrow stage, along the left and right of the playing area; on a wide, shallow stage, along the front and back). No one sits in the "house." This does limit seating, but maintains the feeling of the audience as observers inside a prison.

COSTUMES

For Opening Section: The actors are dressed in the most extreme of the audience's fantasies of how "bad girls" look. At the O M T we used cheap prison novels, the covers of *True Detective* magazines and grade C women's prison movies as prime resources.

For the Body of the Play: The women prisoners were dressed in the simplest cotton housedresses and tennis shoes. When they transform into guards they slip on colorful band uniform jackets. When they transform into the visiting evangelists, they don thrift-shop fashions and "proper" ladies' hats.

ACT ONE

(The play begins. All twinkle lights twinkle up, as do playing area lights. The audio tape is turned off. The actors enter in extreme slow motion. They flirt with, seduce and try every available means to con the spectators. Gradually the audience members become aware of the actors who move toward them. They can only view the actors through the jail cells. Because of the physical setup, the audience has to work to see what is going on. As the actors enter their cells, the slow motion ends and each begins her opening monologue to con. Each actor speaks directly to various audience members trying to convince each one of her innocence.)

(When JOCKEY *begins to speak to the audience, twinkle lights on all cells remain on. Those lights on* JOCKEY*'s cell flash in rhythm to her speech. When* JOCKEY *takes focus, general light comes up on all cells.)*

JOCKEY: Listen! You aren't gonna see what really goes on here. They'll have the whole place—and us—sanitized, de-loused, sterile, perfect and old-time Christian clean. They'll make you very happy with the way your tax dollars are being spent. Their lives depend on that, you bet! But make them show you the hole. They got a hole in here—they call it "The Adjustment Center." They want everything here to sound like a hospital or a school so you'll think that with a new name somethin's changed around here. No matter how many times they call it a "campus," this place is still a joint. You know what happens here? Nothing. Nothing. And then lots more of the same. They taught me how to fill a bucket with water and soap. Where to put my hands on the handle of a mop and how to tell the floor from the walls. When I get out of here, I get to be the best hotel maid in the world—but I'm allergic to detergent. Look at my hands—all the skin is peeling off.

*(The lights continue to twinkle—*RONNIE *and* JOCKEY *are cellmates.)*

RONNIE: Hi. How're you tonight? Welcome to our "campus." It's such a nice drive on a clear day. I get into town often lately. Some groups who're interested in us ask for me to come and speak to them about how we're doing here. And believe me, I'm glad to talk about it. I've come a long way since I got convinced I was my own worst enemy. I was doing hard time. I was so mean I spent forty-nine days in the "Adjustment Center." I wasn't about to change for nobody. But then it dawned on me that the more I stayed in a negative vibration state, the longer it would be till I could get back out into the free world. I just had to turn myself around and become the other side of the coin. For the first six months I had nothing but all the shit jobs—

scrubbing and scrubbing and then rubbing. When it got dry they let me paint it—you know what I mean? But now I've worked my way up to be head clerk of records here. I'm saving my money. I got a bank account. I'm getting skills I could use in an insurance company or any nice, clean business like that. Now I'm doing easy time and looking forward to joining you all one day soon. Loan me a cigarette?

(Twinkle lights come up on CHAMP*'s cell. They remain on around* RONNIE *and* JOCKEY*'s cell.* RONNIE *exits to change to* MISS SCHNAUZER.*)*

CHAMP: Hello? You come with a tour group? Wanna play ball? Got a good team here. El Toro bats three-fifty, and that's on her bad days. Listen, would you ask the Warden if she'll let you take us swimming? I want to see something else. We get tired of looking at each other. You roller skate? I was All Junior Champ in high school. They gave me up to two years for possession. You believe it? Don't you think it's pretty silly to spend all your money keeping me here for two jays? My problem is I didn't think big enough.... They pardon the guys, the really *big* guys. They got respect for the big guys. Us little women, they bust us and throw away the key. I was out riding in the first car I could ever afford to buy myself—had only two jays in my pocket. It was on the way to get my inspection sticker. Lucky it was my first offense or I'd have up to six. Cute, eh? Write your Congressman. I write every day. If you don't have a record, they might even take you seriously. Try it. Costs a hell of a lot of dough to keep me here. I'd rather be surf fishing in San Clemente!

(Lights twinkle around EL TORO*'s cell—stay on, on* CHAMP*'s.)*

EL TORO: Nobody gonna rehabilitate you! You rehabilitate yourself, y'understand? Like, if I'm sitting here and you tell me to sit a certain way and look prim and proper like a lady...I'm not gonna feel like doing that. That ain't me. I like to sit and think, and I don't smile when I'm looking inside, y'understand? Sometimes I get up in the morning, I want to take a walk. I might want to talk to someone. But they don't let you talk to anyone until after one P M on Saturday. They got me trained to wake up at six-thirty A M. *(Laughs, sputters)* I used to go to *bed* at six-thirty A M! They got me working in the sewing shop now, and I like it O K. But when I first came here they couldn't understand me. They don't realize that some of us out there, *we don't work.* Not everybody has to do a nine-to-fiver for chump change, y'understand. They write me up all the time about my attitude. The matron always is looking at me *(Demonstrates)* when I'm like this, see—sitting and tripping on myself—and she says, "What's wrong wit chew? You're not happy!" I'm perfectly happy, *sitting here.* But around here they want you always to be sitting like this *(She demonstrates a super-perfect, little girl pose.)* and grinning like an ape. Otherwise they think you've gone mental! Like this babe we had in here. She set fire to her mattress because they wouldn't let her hold hands with the person she was sweet on. They sent her to California. Told her she'd be happier there. Told her there were no girls here like the "way" she was, y'understand? But there were five hundred of them in the prison in California and she wouldn't have to set fire to her mattress there.

(Lights twinkle around KATHLEEN*'s cell—remain on* EL TORO*'s.)*

KATHLEEN: I wouldn't work in a job where they can keep track of you. You got to be out of your mind, honey. I know what I'm talking about. My poor old mama, she worked in a square job all her life. She worked as a waitress, she worked as a florist. She had a trade, honey. You know what I mean—she was an artist with flowers! When her arthritis got so bad she couldn't make corsages and funeral sprays no more, she went back into waitressing at Dunkin' Donuts. She worked all her life—like since they invented Social Security—you dig? She kept all her forms and she wrote down all her numbers, you dig? She was always up front with her numbers. So she retires two years ago. You know what the government gives her for working from the time she was ten years old—you know what they give her? Seventy-eight dollars a month. Count 'em. Thanks a lot. Working fifty-five years, you dig? Fifty-five years. How's she supposed to live on seventy-eight dollars a month?? You figure it out. She'd be better off in here with us.

(The sound rises fully as all prisoners now join with KATHLEEN*, speaking key phrases from their speeches. All lights twinkle until* MISS SCHNAUZER*, a prison official, appears at opposite end of the playing area. When the women see her, they fall silent and withdraw into their darkened cells. During* MISS SCHNAUZER*'s speech they change to prison dresses and tennis shoes. Over their dresses they wear identical green or blue hospital or prison gowns.* MISS SCHNAUZER *wears a gray and red guard coat. [In the Omaha Magic Theatre production, when prisoners transformed to guards, they slipped into bright marching band uniform jackets.]* MISS SCHNAUZER *unties the rope which has kept the audience confined to the lobby. She shakes some hands, welcoming them into the prison, and directs them to seats. She smiles to both sides of the audience, makes a gesture of welcome, stops, looks down at the floor. She's not used to addressing so many people from the free world at one time. She straightens up, works to relax her body, her eyes showing inner disturbance. As she speaks she scans each audience member very closely. She is checking to see that no contraband [matches, cigarettes, a sharp object, a belt] is brought into the prison. Years of watching for the passing of contraband and/or the tapping of love messages on toes keep her from letting go of the "guard" mind set. She may be any age, but seems youthful and "with it.")*

MISS SCHNAUZER: Hello there—I'm Miss Schnauzer, Assistant to our Warden, in charge of working with the Parole Board, the Legislature, and you—the community—and I want to welcome you to our campus. I think some of you may have noticed the new sign just to the right of the front gate: "WOMEN'S STATE CORRECTIONAL FACILITY." The legislature was kind enough to vote us a new name this year and we were able to paint a new sign with materials left over from repairing our "Adjustment Center."

In the dark ages of penology, there was a place where inmates were confined for punishment, which our charges referred to as "solitary confinement," or euphemistically, as "the hole." But since the sociological-anthropo-sensitivity-psychiatric revolution has brought us into this new age of enlightenment—and thus more humane treatment geared toward rehabilitation—what used to be called "the hole" is now a gaily painted place where inmates who may be feeling upset may go to meditate—alone—away from the *hubbub* of correctional life.

(She crosses to area in front of cells as she speaks. By this time most of the changing activity has been completed—at least all uncovering that the audience shouldn't see. As she crosses, lights follow her. They go out as she passes out of the area.)

MISS SCHNAUZER: As East has met West, we in the West have been wise enough at times, I hope, to gear up and make use of some of the applicable Far Eastern personal development techniques which can be utilized in bringing sanity and calmness to some of our angrier ladies.

(Distant growls and bar rattling noise from the cell areas. MISS SCHNAUZER *waits for it to end. She does not look at inmates but holds a smile on the audience.)*

MISS SCHNAUZER: A few days of meditation and scientifically controlled fasting in "The Adjustment Center" helps a disturbed individual realize she'd rather have the company of her new friends here as well as three square meals a day. Further, I'd like to call your attention to the up-to-date plumbing. No woman has to flush a toilet herself. The flushing is controlled at the central guard station. This way one matron can supervise an entire cottage of girls, where it might have taken up to five before. This saves you, our employers and taxpayers, money in eliminated salaries. I'm really happy you were able to come today, as tensions sometimes run high here and seeing faces from the free world, faces of those who know how to live on the street—I mean in ordinary society—can an act as an inspiration to our girls. As I'm sure you realize, by the time a girl is placed in here she's reached rock bottom. We work hard with the girls to help build up their self images, to teach them a trade so they may one day take their places as useful members of society. You'll hear various stories today. Please take most of them with a grain of salt. A lot of our girls have lived quite unreal lives and they do exaggerate their cases, and the reasons why they are here. But please understand me, we do show compassion for our girls, but not sympathy. You may feel at times that you want to show sympathy toward some of them, but let me caution you in advance: "sympathy is weakness." They won't respect you for it. They'll respect you if you respect them, but "sympathy is weakness," and they'll use every con game in the book to get you to fall for their stories. Thank you again for coming and showing an interest in what we're trying to do. We do need more money for staff and better facilities and you can help us toward these with your vote. And now we'll show you a composite picture of a day in the life of our facility. Please don't feed the inmates or ask to eat with us. Our budget doesn't cover you.

*(*MISS SCHNAUZER *breaks into an enormous, toothy smile which freezes on her face. She rotates so that all the audience partakes of her good will. One prisoner comes out of her cell transformed to a* GUARD *wearing a blue and red jacket. She marches toward* MISS SCHNAUZER, *who stands smiling and rotating. They perform a military "changing of the guard." The new* GUARD *lifts a violin to her shoulder and plays a dissonant chord to signify the prison bell. At sound of the chord, twinkle lights come up on cells and prisoners press noses to cell bars for count. Each prisoner, in an order established by the director, calls out a number from one to forty. These numbers vary from count to count.)*

JOCKEY: Two

OX TAIL: Seven.

CHAMP: Sixteen.

EL TORO: Twenty-eight.

RONNIE: Thirty-six.

KATHLEEN: Forty.

*(*GUARD *marches to cells and unlocks doors. [In Omaha Magic Theatre's production this was signified by hitting cell bars with a chain.] The prisoners [except* KATHLEEN, *who has been restricted] come out of their cells, stretching and yawning.* GUARD *moves to center playing area and mimes turning on showers. [In O M T's production the prisoners wore green surgical gowns as robes over their other costumes.] As they wait for their showers, the* GUARD *drags* KATHLEEN *from her cell and takes her to a shower way from the other women. During the following scene this* GUARD *takes a great deal of interest in* KATHLEEN*'s shower. Periodically,* KATHLEEN *will catch the* GUARD *in the act of looking her up and down. The* GUARD *looks away just before their eyes meet. The other prisoners mime taking their showers [they do not remove their clothes].* RONNIE *showers with the rest, but listens and does not speak.)*

(Under the showers:)

EL TORO: Got any kids?

CHAMP: Four. You?

EL TORO: Had two, but only know where one is.

JOCKEY: I got two. What happened to the other?

EL TORO: I don't know.

CHAMP: When'd you have it?

EL TORO: Reform school. I know it was alive. Right after birth I held her just for a minute. But then they knocked me out with something, and when I came to, they told me the baby died. I still don't believe them.

CHAMP: Awww, they adopted it out, I bet.

JOCKEY: Probably sold it.

CYNTHIA: Yeah, I heard of 'em doing that.

EL TORO: I've got my Ma, and a volunteer lawyer trying to track her down. I know in my heart she's alive.

JOCKEY: You saw her alive?

EL TORO: That's how come I know she was a girl.

(She winks at CHAMP, *beckons her to join in her joke on* JOCKEY*—they both sneak up on* JOCKEY*)*

EL TORO: She was so beautiful...when she was born the doctor threw her up on my breast... *(Directly behind* JOCKEY*)* ...and she went right for the nipple!

(They grab JOCKEY*'s breast.)*

JOCKEY: *(Shocked, then laughing)* That's a girl all right!

(All in shower laugh. MATRON *becomes vaguely aware of the disturbance. She has been totally submerged in her action with* KATHLEEN. EL TORO *immediately acts as if she is comforting* JOCKEY, *who immediately acts as if she's ill.* CHAMP *acts normal, keeps showering as her cover.)*

MATRON: All right, keep it down—you're turnin' into prunes.

*(*MATRON *takes* KATHLEEN *from the shower [she was clearly not finished showering] and places her in solitary confinement behind the net.* KATHLEEN *looks for a way out, finds methods of making the time pass during her stay behind "the net." The prisoners finish their showers and dress.* JOCKEY *and* EL TORO *dress, while in line with the others,* JOCKEY *in front of* EL TORO.*)*

JOCKEY: Don't get butch with me—we're not home.

EL TORO: Since when I live at yer house?

JOCKEY: Whatcha got, a hormone rush?

EL TORO: I washed my hands and I can't do a thing with 'em.
(Runs fingers up and down JOCKEY*'s body.)*

JOCKEY: I'll have ta get butch and beat yer ass.

EL TORO: *(Bumping buns)* We could go to different holes together.

JOCKEY: Who ya been takin' butch lessons from?

EL TORO: Not from you, you bum fuck! *(Sticks out tongue)*

JOCKEY: *(Grabs tongue)* You stick that out, ya got to use it.

EL TORO: Why, Miss Butch, you flirting with me?

(The violin/bell sounds, women line up for the count. They measure an arm's length between them and begin:)

JOCKEY: Six.

RONNIE: Thirteen.

CHAMP: Fifteen.

EL TORO: Twenty-seven.

KATHLEEN: Thirty.

(The prisoners move to scrub the floor. As they scrub, RONNIE *transforms into* MATRON ONE, CYNTHIA *into* MATRON TWO. *They stand back to back—they keep watch. Their eyes dart from prisoner to prisoner, from one audience member to another, checking for disruptions and contraband. They move, still back to back, in a circle as they speak.)*

MATRON ONE: It's a clear day.

MATRON TWO: Not a cloud.

MATRON ONE: Did you hear about Lieutenant Meeker?

MATRON TWO: What?

MATRON ONE: Totaled her car last night.

MATRON TWO: Oh, no.

MATRON ONE: Yeah, can't save it.

MATRON TWO: That car was a classic.

MATRON ONE: I always told her if she hung on to it, she'd get five thousand for it in about twenty years.

MATRON TWO: I saw an article in *Time* that they're selling old cars down in Austin for fifty to eighty thousand.

MATRON ONE: I saw that, too.

MATRON TWO: My Dad had a truck come and haul his Oldsmobile away two years ago.

MATRON ONE: The one with the fins?

MATRON TWO: That's the one.

MATRON ONE: How much is it worth now?

MATRON TWO: Aw, they squashed it into a cube and sold it for scrap, but if it was in running order, I figure Dad coulda sold it for thirty thousand in about twenty years. There wasn't a dent in it and the chrome was perfect.

MATRON ONE: No rust?

MATRON TWO: Not that I noticed.

(MATRON ONE *plays violin/belt sound. Women line up for count.)*

JOCKEY: Seven.

CHAMP: Ten.

EL TORO: Sixteen.

KATHLEEN: Twenty-eight.

MATRON TWO: Specified women report to the sewing room... *(Going down line at random)* You...you...YOU...you...

(If company size allows, MATRON TWO *oversees workers in sewing room. The women who were picked move on to the sewing room where they pantomime folding and ironing sheets. As this happens,* EL TORO *and* JOCKEY *move to the net to tell* KATHLEEN *that they weren't able to get her the contraband [valium] they had promised her. Whispers—discussion ensues. A* MATRON *intervenes. If company is small,* MATRON TWO *transforms back into* CYNTHIA *for work in the sewing room.)*

MATRON: No talking.

EL TORO: *(Innocent)* Just saying hello.

MATRON: You know the rules.

EL TORO: What's wrong with hello?

MATRON: Nothing. Hello, El Toro. You're elected to scrub this hall.

(Kicks her behind the knee, forcing EL TORO *to the floor.)*

EL TORO: But I just scrubbed it this morning.

MATRON: It's dirty from all the hellos. Every time you say hello, El Toro, you say it so juicy you get spit on my clean floor. Down on your knees.

(Notices JOCKEY *still talking quietly to* KATHLEEN*)*

MATRON: You, too. You there.

JOCKEY: Me?

MATRON: You, lady. Down and scrub.

(Hands mop to JOCKEY, *sponge and bucket to* EL TORO.*)*

MATRON: Learn to be a good little housekeeper and you can get a first-class man when you get out. Real good housekeepers are careful of their work.

*(Points out blemishes on floor—*JOCKEY *follows her around and scrubs.)*

MATRON: There's a spot, and there's a spot.

(Finds one in front of EL TORO.*)*

EL TORO: That's your shadow.

MATRON: Why, so it is.

(Kicks bucket, drenching EL TORO *with water.)*

MATRON: And my shadow just kicked the bucket. Hurry it up, don't let the water get into the cells, or you'll be mopping all week. *(Marching)* Faster, faster. No man would put up with such a slow wife, ladies. Elbow grease, that's what my Granddad said it takes—elbow grease.

(Gritting their teeth, the two women work as fast as possible to mop up the water.)

(Scene Five is the sewing room—circle of light in front of the cells. The prisoners mime folding and ironing sheets and pillowcases. Two MATRONS *are supervising.* MATRON TWO *is the instructor or overseer of the work.* MATRON ONE *has just entered. She stands in front of the net, checks out and collects the tools of the work. This scene is to be done with easy familiarity and playfulness.)*

CHAMP: Another day, another two-and-a-half cents from "Sam."

JOCKEY: *(Comes into the sewing room after scrubbing the floor)* Minus two, ya mean.

ALL: Yeah, you can say that again. I know what you mean. *(Et cetera)*

JOCKEY: Yeah, man, when I get out, I'm gonna buy a Silver Cloud Rolls Royce with all the millions I'm earning in this joint.

*(*EL TORO *has come in from scrubbing floors, folds sheets with* JOCKEY.*)*

OX TAIL: You'll be lucky if you can buy one skate.

EL TORO: Can't afford a skate key, I'm so in debt.

OX TAIL: You owe me seven cartons of cigarettes. Be rest of your life paying off.

EL TORO: Ah, c'mon baby, take it out in trade.

OX TAIL: Since ya asked me nice.

CHAMP: *(To* MATRON ONE*)* I saw the way you smiled at Mrs Snowden.

MATRON ONE: I'm feeling good today.

JOCKEY: You're always feeling good when you're near Mrs Snowden.

(The others laugh. MATRON ONE *blushes.)*

OX TAIL: Hey, look, Mrs Beecroft is blushing.

MATRON TWO: Keep it down to a dull roar. Let's get the work out, okay?

EL TORO: She's sweet on Snowden.

MATRON ONE: My husband would be interested to hear that.

CHAMP: What he don't know won't hurt him.

MATRON ONE: Okay, cut the kidding.

JOCKEY: Kidding? Who's kidding?

EL TORO: And they put us in the hole for getting married.

MATRON ONE: Come on, hurry it up or I'll have to write you up.

JOCKEY: Yer cute when yer mad.

MATRON TWO: You listen to too many movies.

OX TAIL: She don't "watch" 'em, that's for sure.

JOCKEY: Would be the waste of a good movie.

CHAMP: Hey, Mrs Beecroft, can I call you up for a date when I get out of here?

MATRON ONE: You'll never get out of here if you spend all your time on love affairs.

CHAMP: Affairs? Affairs? I'm a fine, upstanding, married Christian woman with two children.

OX TAIL: And three wives.

(They all laugh.)

EL TORO: No, she's only got two. One lucked out of here last week.

MATRON ONE: I didn't hear any crying.

CHAMP: This joint is a supermarket and all the tomatoes are free.

OX TAIL: Mrs Snowden is looking at Mrs Beecroft, now.

MATRON TWO: To signal her to write you up for distracting four people from doing their work. *(She says this with warmth.)*

OX TAIL: Yer an all-right chick, Mrs Beecroft—

MATRON ONE: Woman, not chick.

OX TAIL: That matron on the night shift is some kind of bitch—I mean witch. She makes us obey rules that haven't even been invented yet.

*(*MATRON ONE *crosses to play dissonant chord on violin [the "bell" sound]. Prisoners line up for a count.* MATRON TWO *transforms back to* CYNTHIA.*)*

JOCKEY: Three.

CYNTHIA: Eleven.

CHAMP: Fifteen.

OX TAIL: Twenty-two.

EL TORO: Twenty-nine.

KATHLEEN: *(From net)* Thirty-six.

*(*OX TAIL *transforms into* HEAD MATRON. *Other prisoners are still in line.)*

MATRON ONE: They're bringing in a new load of prisoners.

*(*MATRON ONE *crosses to cell, unlocks door [at O M T, rattles chain].* HEAD MATRON *crosses to net, grabs* KATHLEEN, *who transforms into a new prisoner and is walked across the playing area and thrown in cell. The prisoners get very excited as they watch the new ones come in.)*

EL TORO: Fresh fish!

JOCKEY: Hot zucchini!

(They continue to cat-call and comment on the women: they might have known "that one" from high school or "that one" from a recent local T V show. This banter continues until KATHLEEN *and* MATRON *pass—then each woman in count line transforms into a* NEW PRISONER *as* KATHLEEN *and* MATRON *pass her. Some of the women may show signs of fatigue and pain from various forms of drug addiction. Others may be jumpy and irritable from heavy drinking. Some may still bear bruises and other marks of their "apprehension" [i.e., forcible arrest]. Certain "political prisoners" may be recovering from severe burns on arms, legs, heads or faces [i.e., from being burned out of hideouts by police] or gunshot wounds. Some may be "spaced out" from past heavy drug usage; others may be cool and keep to themselves, or some are easygoing, but show no "heavy" emotion.* MATRON ONE *transforms into a new arrival and joins the others who are moved en masse by the* HEAD MATRON *across the playing area toward the net. The image the actors project during this move is one of animals being led to slaughter, done in silence, very slowly.)*

HEAD MATRON: All right ladies, right this way.

(Takes a prisoner by the arm and leads her to a place behind the net)

HEAD MATRON: Nice to see you so bright this early.

(Sends another prisoner to the net)

HEAD MATRON: Step up to the counter and verify the list of your belongings.

(Leads another prisoner)

HEAD MATRON: This is the last time you'll see them till you get out.

(Takes another prisoner out of line)

HEAD MATRON: If it isn't on the list now, it won't be there when you go home.

(Sends last prisoner to the net)

(All the NEW PRISONERS *are now lined up behind the net. They are captive there.)*

EL TORO: *(Intimately, without moving)* I feel like I've known you all my life.

JOCKEY: Me, too.

EL TORO: Who are you?

JOCKEY: A messenger.

EL TORO: What for?

JOCKEY: To make you happy. *(Leans to kiss her)*

(In the following section two speakers at a time say the same lines, but with their own rhythms and intentions. In this way, it becomes a jam. KATHLEEN *speaks to* EL TORO *across the space between the cells and the net.* CHAMP *and* CYNTHIA *speak intimately to each other without moving—they are behind the net.)*

KATHLEEN & CHAMP: I need something.

EL TORO & CYNTHIA: I know what you need.

KATHLEEN & CHAMP: How do you know it?

EL TORO & CYNTHIA: Been watching you.

KATHLEEN & CHAMP: I been watching you, too.

EL TORO & CYNTHIA: I want to lay my head down on your breast.

KATHLEEN & CHAMP: C'mere.

(During the following confrontation, the other PRISONERS *behind the net quietly begin to " look for a way out."* ALL PRISONERS *[including* KATHLEEN *in the cell] participate except* RONNIE. *This continues throughout the scene. The* MATRON *maintains her distance, speaks from in front of cells toward* RONNIE, *who stands at the side of the net.)*

MATRON: What have you got in your hand?

RONNIE: Nothin'.

MATRON: I saw something flash!

RONNIE: Far out. *(Looks around)* Where?

MATRON: Don't be smart. Act like a lady.

RONNIE: If I did you'd arrest me all over again. Ladies are prostitutes, and I never hooked in my....

MATRON: Ladies are ladies, and ladies get respect.

RONNIE: Not where I come from.

MATRON: Hold out your hand or be ready to go before the disciplinary committee.

RONNIE: *(Reluctantly holds out her hand)* Yes, ma'am.

MATRON: A salt shaker?

RONNIE: Hey, you guessed it.

MATRON: That's enough.

(RONNIE *drops imaginary shaker)*

MATRON: Why'd you take it?

RONNIE: T' brighten up m' room.

MATRON: A salt shaker?

RONNIE: Different strokes for different folks.

MATRON: I'll have to report this.

RONNIE: *(Pleading now, her kidding attitude gone)* Aww, please, Mrs Frank, give me a break? I hardly knew I walked out of the dining room with it—it's just it was shiny, and it's so drab here.

MATRON: Smarten up! *(Mimes writing something in a little book)* All right, ladies, you will now line up and strip to your shoes and socks.

(The PRISONERS *come out from behind the net, stand in a straight line in front of it. As they do,* JOCKEY *unrolls a sheet of white paper that is attached to two poles and stretches it to the other end of the platform attaching other pole to metal holders on side of platform, thus making a scrim that covers the women from neck to mid-thigh. A light behind the net is turned on and other lights dimmed so the stripping can be seen in silhouette. The* WOMEN *strip to socks and shoes.)*

MATRON: Hand all your clothes to the inmate who's checked your belongings list and your clothing will be added to it. Your new ensemble will be provided by the State.

(Articles of clothing [at O M T the green surgical robes] are passed down the line toward JOCKEY, *at far end of line. New clothing [men's hats and sports jackets] are passed up the line. The* PRISONERS *mime dressing. They put on sport coats as they would dresses—wiggle into them, zip...they hold hats.)*

MATRON: Roll your underwear and other garments up and hand them to the personnel you see here. Speed it up. We have to get on to your space assignments.

*(*EL TORO *stands motionless, looking at dress [really a sports jacket but it's behind white paper]. The* HEAD MATRON *addresses her.)*

MATRON: What's the matter? Get dressed.

EL TORO: I never wore no dress before.

*(*HEAD MATRON *crosses to lineup, looks under the white paper, crosses away and takes line.)*

MATRON: You're a female, I see. That means you'll wear a dress here.

EL TORO: I don't think I can, Ma'am.

MATRON: You'll address me as Lieutenant Meeker.

EL TORO: I can't wear no dress, Lieutenant Meeker.

MATRON: You asking for the hole?

EL TORO: I'm sorry, Lieutenant Meeker, but it will make me sick to wear a dress.

MATRON: You have ten seconds to get it on. *(Looks at watch)* One, two, three, four, five...

*(*EL TORO *awkwardly pulls dress [sport coat] on and stands there, mortified.)*

MATRON: There now, you look real cute in that. Nobody dies from wearing dresses...

*(*EL TORO *faints in place. The other* PRISONERS *catch her, try to revive her.)*

MATRON: On your feet. You're holding up the parade.

(Other PRISONERS *pull* EL TORO *up)*

MATRON: *(Quieting them down, regaining control)* All right, ladies, you will now pledge allegiance.

(All jump to attention, put their hands to hearts)

MATRON: We will sing our new, special "Fight Depression" song, so thoughtfully written by our own Miss Schnauzer's grandfather.

(The women burst through the paper screen, wearing men's hats and sports jackets over their dresses. HEAD MATRON *transforms back into* OX TAIL. *She wears sports jacket under guard coat which she removes and joins the others. The subtext of this song is the prisoners' fantasy of themselves as pop-art criminals.)*

PRISONERS: *(Sing)* Tighten your belt and
Tough it out.
Some lamebrains born
On the prairies,
Or in the smog-soaked
Basins;
Starved into
Staring awareness,
And suspicious
Short-order cooks
By the Depression—the
"Great Depression" that is—
Have stuffed their faith
Up in holy argyle socks and
Play a loner's game;
Sneaking
On slippery dewy limbs
Fall into spider nets
Saying "I know exactly where I am
At all times. I planned it. I planned it."
I'm the best damn Sunday morning quarterback
Who ever lived
And if you doubt it, I'll
Start phoning you long distance
At three o'clock in the morning.
My goal-posts are always up
And painted day-glow white.
That's right!
I never sleep
Because I keep
An open eye
On history.
Thirty thousand years from now
I want to see it written—"He sold Orange

Julius to the Chinese,
Quadraphonic to the Sudanese,
A *(Insert two-syllable name of local fast food store—i. e., McDonald's or Dairy Queen)* on every
Kremlin corner.
Arabs drive Continentals,
While Saddam sleeps
Steely eyed wide
On a Sealy Posturepedic.
Chilean–Brazilian generals reside in
Amphibious Cadillacs,
Hubcaps engraved
With images of doves who
Carry Picasso's eyes
Blazing in their talons."

(The WOMEN *peel off their sports coats. The next three lines are said simultaneously as* KATHLEEN *goes back to her cell,* RONNIE *and the other* PRISONERS *go back behind the net.* EL TORO *remains in the central playing area.)*

EL TORO: The first time I tried to kill myself...

RONNIE: I tried to kill myself lots of times.

KATHLEEN: I tried to kill myself three times.

EL TORO: *(Alone in the center space addresses audience)* ...I waited till everyone was gone to work... *(Stops suddenly, looks around, relives fantasy of what it was like to be out on the streets. She feels she is being followed by something. When she is sure she is no longer followed, she continues. This continues throughout the scene in places indicated)* ...then I got this Japanese carbine that my Dad brought back from the South Pacific... *(Stops, looks around, waits, goes on)* ...and I went into the hall closet with it. *(Takes a breath, looks around, continues)* First I tried to put the barrel of the gun to my temple, but the closet was too small for that. *(Stops, looks, waits, goes on)* So then I remember reading a story in the *Enquirer* about how this guy had blown his head off by putting this shotgun in his mouth—*(Inhales deeply as she says)*-so-o-o-o-o-o-o-o-o-o-o-, *(Shapes her hand like a pistol, sticks the barrel in her mouth, rotates in a circle with this image so the audience can see, curls up in a ball on the floor)* And I pulled the trigger.

RONNIE: *(From the net)* But I never had enough pills to keep me out more than twenty-four hours. Except for the time they kept me in the hole for three months—I lost my mind.

*(*JOCKEY *transforms into* MATRON THREE, *puts on guard coat, pushes cart center; crosses to pull* RONNIE *from behind net and places her in cart,* EL TORO *continues speaking and moving all around center area. The cart is solitary confinement, a cell on wheels that is moved up and down the center space by* MATRON THREE. RONNIE *tries desperately to get out. She scratches messages on the floor with her fingernails, bangs her head against the bars.)*

EL TORO: *(From floor)* It tasted of oil, and lint... *(Rises)* ...and shit. *(Stops abruptly, looks around, listens, relaxes, goes on)* ...Then I realized I needed a shell for the gun, but it was a Jap gun, and none of the shells around the house would fit it. I got so mad I threw the gun down, and I decided I'd have to move out since I couldn't find nothing to use to kill myself. From that day on I was a lot happier—all I had to do was move out. Why did it take me so long to find that out?

*(*MATRON THREE *crosses to* KATHLEEN *in cell—she is being prepared for a medical examination.)*

EL TORO: If it's rotten you move—simple as that. Pack up and move out. *(Joins others behind the net)*

MATRON THREE: *(To* KATHLEEN*)* Give me your bra.

KATHLEEN: Watch out, it'll burn ya.

MATRON THREE: No talking. One more wisecrack and you go to the hole.

*(*KATHLEEN *opens her mouth, then closes it.)*

MATRON THREE: Shoes, cigarettes, wristwatch, rings.

(Reaching out from cell to MATRON *like a balancing act,* KATHLEEN *offers some part of her body—leg, heart, neck—as each item is called for.)*

MATRON THREE: Get up on the table and prepare for your enema.

*(*KATHLEEN *looks at her, sneers and shrugs.)*

RONNIE: *(From solitary where she's been pounding on floor to find a loose board. She rattles bars—the* MATRONS *who guard her are expressionless and unhearing. They or* MATRON THREE *turn the cart in a circular fashion in the center area.)* Let me out of here! You evil bastard bitches—your hair is on fire, and snakes with blazing fangs live between yer yellow teeth—I seen 'em, I seen 'em. Let me out of here. You hear me! You stinkin' shitheads, ya motherfuckin' dirty daughters of the Jesus lickers—I tell you once and for all, let me out of here! I'll kick this place in and tear you limb from limb, *(Climbs to highest point of cart rail)* and use yer ribs to spear yer hearts, you farts! *(Standing free on top rail)* You can't keep me in here—I won't stay in here!—Don't you know who I am? You let me out of here right now, you sinning, grinning, stuffed-assed satans. *(Jumps down)* Let me out! Right now! I command you! Let me out! *(Continues "Let me out!" as a demand, a plea, beating herself up, etc.)* Let me out! Let me out of here! *(Looks for a way out)*

*(*RONNIE*'s chanting of "Let me out!" incites supportive outcries from the other* WOMEN *behind the net. This becomes a jam of different intentions for the "Let me out!" outcry. It continues through the next three speeches.)*

KATHLEEN: *(From the cells—comes right in overlapping "Let me out...!")* I really didn't know who I was—I just knew I couldn't take the pain any more. I felt like the sharpest axe was wedged right down my head between my eyes and sinking lower every minute—every single minute the axe was cutting me. It would get to the bottom of my brain, and then another axe would start at the top of my head and slice right down beside the first axe. Not in the same place, but like slicing salami, neat and in a row. The pain of the slicing kept right on. Let me out!

RONNIE: Let me out!

ALL PRISONERS: Let me out!

CYNTHIA: *(Jumps out from behind net to immediately in front of it)* I didn't have no clothes—only a blood-soaked, pissed-out mattress, and a hole in the floor—and it was so cold, the cold ate at my hands and toes as sharp as the axe in my head.

*(Lunges and throws herself on cart—*MATRON *shakes her loose.)*

CYNTHIA: I turned into an animal, but smart. *(Mimes picking up spoon from floor, threatens audience.)* I kept a spoon. I told them it had fallen down the shit hole, and I sharpened that spoon—I made that spoon so sharp I could cut my hair with it. Then when it got sharp enough, I lay down on the cold cement floor and I cut both my wrists. Let me out! *(Lies flat on floor)*

RONNIE: Let me out!

KATHLEEN: Let me out!

CHAMP: *(Comes out from behind net to floor)* I can't tell you what a great feeling that was—the pain started to run out of my head, *(Lowers herself onto* CYNTHIA*'s body)* right onto the floor. And I was beginning to relax at last, feeling the pressure just sigh right on out of me. *(Sits up—jam of "Let me out!" stops.)* I'd been waiting and waiting and waiting for that feeling. See—*(Shows the audience a real scar)*—here's the scar. See there?

(Each WOMAN *shows one member of the audience a scar she has on her wrist, arm, face, neck, etc. saying:)*

EACH PRISONER: See? See there?

*(*ALL WOMEN *enter the solitary cell [the cart]. They mime being chained to it by their wrists and pivot in a circle in the center area [at O M T* JOCKEY *pushed with one foot while* OX TAIL *walked it around—she is tethered to the rail of the cart like ox in a yoke]. They testify to the pain of their situation with their hands.)*

RONNIE: *(In midst of the others)* But they put me in the hospital and sewed me up. I was so mad they brought me back, I tried to throw things at the nurses. I pulled the tubes out of my arms, but they just kept putting them back. It was so beautiful to die, just like I thought it would be. It was so warm, and my grandmother was waiting for me with her arms out like this—and just as I was going to run into her arms they brought me back. After I healed up they put me back in the hole. I had to eat with my fingers—they wouldn't give me no spoons.

*(*RONNIE *joins others in testifying with their hands tied to the rail of the cart. The* PRISONERS *sing in harmony.)*

PRISONERS: Jesus walked
This lonesome valley.
He had to walk
It by himself.
Oh, nobody else
Could walk it for him.
He had to walk it by himself.
We must walk
This lonesome valley.
We have to walk
It by ourselves.
Oh, nobody else
Can walk it for us.
We have to walk it by ourselves.

(They break out of the cart, move to positions across playing area, and taking a vigorous, positive attitude, sing the song as a joyous gospel.)

PRISONERS: You "gotta go"
And stand your trial.
You "gotta go"
And stand it by yourself.
Oh, nobody else
Can stand it for you.
You gotta go and stand it by yourself
Yourself!

*(*EL TORO *drops to her knees and begins to scrub toward center of the playing area. From the opposite end of the playing area,* CYNTHIA *scrubs toward her, closer and closer to her. She stares at* EL TORO*, smiles, tries to catch her eye, clears her throat or lets her brush get away from her so that they somehow touch or get very close.)*

CYNTHIA: *(Very quietly)* I know who you are.

*(*EL TORO *freezes.)*

CYNTHIA: Don't worry. Lotsa people love you.

*(*EL TORO *slowly but deliberately scrubs away from her.)*

CYNTHIA: Really, don't worry. I'm not gonna blow yer cover.

(In a rage, JOCKEY *charges across the floor.)*

JOCKEY: *(Points roughly at* CYNTHIA*)* I'm gonna get you—

(To two other PRISONERS *walking across the space)*

JOCKEY: —and then I'm gonna get *you*—and then *(To* EL TORO*)* I'm gonna get you.

CYNTHIA: *(Stands between* JOCKEY *and* EL TORO*)* Oh no yer not, because first ya gotta go through me.

*(*JOCKEY *shoves* CYNTHIA *away, grabs* EL TORO *by the collar and starts to knock her around*—EL TORO *starts to laugh.)*

EL TORO: Keep it up and one day you might connect.

JOCKEY: *(Frustrated)* You told Betsie you were going to take Dana away from me.

EL TORO: Nobody can take anyone unless they're ready to go.

JOCKEY: *(Lunges at* EL TORO*)* You bitch!

EL TORO: *(Freeing herself)* Butch—that's *butch.*

CYNTHIA: *(Cracking up)* Ya don't wanna get all messed...

JOCKEY: I'm gonna fix yer mouth so's you won't be able to ever eat again, let alone kiss anyone. *(Lunges at* EL TORO*)*

EL TORO: *(Playing with* JOCKEY*)* Keep holding my collar just like that.

(They dance together.)

EL TORO: Yes, that's it, a perfect tilt to the chin and a one and a two and a...

*(*EL TORO *lets* JOCKEY *have it. On the way down,* JOCKEY *snatches* EL TORO*'s glasses and smashes them.)*

JOCKEY: *(Threatening)* I'll put out yer eyes, you creep, you twerp. You can't move in on me.

EL TORO: *(Standing ground)* Give me back my glasses, you motherfucker, or I'll sit on your rotten guts till they burst that yellow shit out all over our nice clean floor.

CYNTHIA: *(Taking* EL TORO *by the hand)* Let's get the fuck outa here.

EL TORO: *(Resisting)* I want her head—I'm gonna blast it open. She's got my glasses.

*(*JOCKEY, EL TORO *and* CYNTHIA *run out.)*

RONNIE: *(She's been keeping watch from cell)* Run. We'll get it. Come on.

(In the cells KATHLEEN, RONNIE *[whose "code" name is* GARY*],* CHAMP *and* JOCKEY *are talking.* KATHLEEN *and* RONNIE *are in one cell,* CHAMP *and* JOCKEY *in another. The rest of the women transform into other* PRISONERS. *The transformation is seen through changes in their walks as they move through the yard, to the warden's office, or back to their cells. With each new walk, the* PRISONERS *give themselves a new destination.)*

KATHLEEN: What's wrong?

GARY: Nothin'.

KATHLEEN: *(Hugging her)* What you mean, nothin'? Tears streaming down your face all morning.

CHAMP: She's always blue about something.

GARY: *(Shaking* KATHLEEN *off)* It's my anniversary.

CHAMP: Why, you should be happy.

KATHLEEN: Yeah—I don't have anniversaries. I wish I had an anniversary. I done broke up with everyone!

GARY: Not mine you wouldn't.

JOCKEY: *(To* CHAMP*)* It's the anniversary of her coming out of the closet.

CHAMP: Yeah, you can still see the splinters in her fists, where she was pounding on the door.

(JOCKEY *and* CHAMP *hit each other and laugh and laugh.)*

GARY: You two are so tough, you miss out on really feeling anything.

KATHLEEN: *(Approaching gently)* Aw, don't mind them—they just like to show off. *(Embracing her)* Are you in love, honey.

GARY: Oh yes. I love a strong man. He stood up to the whole world. He taught me how to take it. I can do easy time because of him. I know I'm going to see him again. Today's our anniversary. Two weeks ago the pigs shot him.

KATHLEEN: *(Holding* GARY*)* Oh honey, I'm so sorry.

CHAMP: *(To* KATHLEEN*)* You gonna fall for that?

JOCKEY: *(To* CHAMP*)* Kick it off—don't hurt her more. You're as bad as the pigs.

CHAMP: *(Pulling up her fist and threatening* JOCKEY*)* Take that back.

JOCKEY: Simmer down.

(CHAMP *and* JOCKEY *wrestle in cell.)*

GARY: *(At* CHAMP *and* JOCKEY*)* You are as bad as the pigs. Fight and shoot, shoot and fight.

CHAMP: *(Pinning* JOCKEY *to the floor)* You're lying.

GARY: It's my anniversary.

CHAMP: Anniversary of your biggest lie.

GARY: I'm not lying.

CHAMP: *(Gets up, moves to bars)* Yea, you are. When I got here you told me your name was Tania.

GARY: Shut up.

CHAMP: You name isn't Tania, is it?

GARY: That was one of my names. But you're not to say it out loud.

CHAMP: You want to know her new code name? It's Gary. Who ever heard of a femme calling herself Gary Gilmore.

(KATHLEEN, *who has continued to try to comfort* GARY, *backs off.)*

GARY: *(No longer looking at* CHAMP*)* I'm calling you crazy. No one would do that.

CHAMP: *(To others)* She told me in the shower her new name was Gary.

GARY: They shot him. He wanted me to go with him.

CHAMP: Tell the others you made it up.

GARY: You're too coarse to understand. It's between his spirit and mine.

CHAMP: There ain't nothin' between you and him but six feet of dirt.

GARY: He lives through me.

CHAMP: He was shot at sunrise.

GARY: I took his name to keep him alive.

CHAMP: *(Swings out of her cell, struts across yard)* Don't you wish you'd met him, baby. You never met a bad-ass like that. The most you ever had was a toothless Hell's Angel who stole you away from your Granddaddy's trailer camp. *(Turns to* RONNIE /GARY *and mocks her.)* He shoved his tongue in your ear when he stole you away and you fell madly in love with his gun and his bike—ain't that right?

(RONNIE/GARY *jumps from her cell and goes after* CHAMP.)

GARY: You bitch!

CHAMP: *(Trying to hold her off)* See what I mean. Holier Than Thou! Look at this wildcat.

GARY: I'm him and he's me, now.

CHAMP: Next thing you'll be Hanoi Hannah and Tokyo Rose.

GARY: They pardoned her, you dope.

CHAMP: You're the dope, you doped-out nut.

GARY: *(Pulling self away)* You're so square you don't know nothing—you're only Champ. I can be as many people as I want to be.

CHAMP: *(To audience and other* PRISONERS*)* See what I mean. She makes her life up out of the T V news.

GARY: *(Lunges at her)* You make your life up out of comic books.

CHAMP: There's a difference?

(They fight fiercely, rolling around on the floor, scratching and kicking. The other PRISONERS *stop and watch, cheer for one or the other, or keep walking so as not to get involved.)*

GARY: *(During the fight)* I'm in love. I'm in love with the whole world.

(They continue to fight ferociously. The WARDEN*'s voice comes over the loudspeaker.)*

WARDEN: Ladies!

*(*RONNIE *and* CHAMP *and all* PRISONERS *freeze, look toward voice and listen.)*

WARDEN: Ladies!

*(*RONNIE *and* CHAMP *separate as if nothing had been going on.)*

WARDEN: Please proceed to your cells.

*(*PRISONERS *run to the cells from wherever they are. They move from cell to cell, cleaning, stashing contraband. Twinkle lights flash as the* WARDEN *continues.)*

WARDEN: Dress appropriately for Sunday worship. Today we will be graced by a visit from the Pentecostal Church. Cells must be cleaned and left in pristine condition as if the Legislature were visiting us. Remember, you are Christian Ladies who keep your houses Christian clean. Your room and your person are reflections of what is going on inside. If you have a messy room or present a messy person, what can anyone think but that your head is a mess...

*(*PRISONERS *run to area in front of net, Put on "Ladies" hats and transform into members of the Pentecostal Church)*

WARDEN:... and therefore, a perfect workshop for the Devil? Ladies, give thought to cleanliness, dress in your Sunday best, and then proceed to the chapel. Give our visitors your undivided attention. They've come a long way to bring us Good News.

(The area in front of net is suddenly bathed in bright light. The piano, accordion or violin begins to play church chords. The Pentecostal CHURCH MEMBERS *are huddled together, terrified of the* PRISONERS. RONNIE *has transformed into the* HEAD WOMAN *who gives the others strength and sends them into the jail to spread the good word as she speaks.)*

HEAD WOMAN: *(Church chords continue under her speech.)* You are in the funhouse...

(She holds OX TAIL*, one of the parishioners, who goes bravely into the prison)*

HEAD WOMAN: ...of the Lord.

(Touches two more women, EL TORO *and* CYNTHIA*, who receive strength and go forth bravely)*

HEAD WOMAN: But be very careful...

(Gives strength to another woman, JOCKEY, *who moves onto the floor)*

HEAD WOMAN: ...that you do not make fun of the Holy Ghost.

(Holds CHAMP *and sends her off)*

(The PENTECOSTALS *are gathered together in the center playing area. They are less terrified after being reassured by the* HEAD WOMAN, *but they still hold onto one another while reaching out to the* PRISONERS *[at O M T the audience became the* PRISONERS *in the actors' minds at this point] to spread the faith for their salvation.)*

ALL PARISHIONERS: *(Sing)*
Even if you don't know how to pray
The ghost within you does.
Listen
Listen
Listen
Listen.
Let the maimed ape have her say.
Let your English mind
Get lost, go blind—;
Take the plunge and speak in tongues.
Mother song
And father sound,
Take the plunge
And speak in tongues.
Listen
Listen
Listen.

(During the second verse of Speak in Tongues, CYNTHIA *and* RONNIE *as* PARISHIONERS *come together center. They are excited.* OX TAIL *and* EL TORO *continue to sing and preach—they have clearly taken the role of Pentecostal ministers. The* MINISTERS *sense the new excitement—they direct their energies to* CYNTHIA *and* RONNIE, *who separate and begin to look inward.)*

JOCKEY, KATHLEEN, EL TORO & CHAMP: *(Sing as* PARISHIONERS*)*
Even if you don't know how to pray
The ghost within you does.

OX TAIL: *(As* MINISTER *directs energy toward* RONNIE*)*
Listen
Listen
Listen
*(*OX TAIL *touches* RONNIE.*)*
Let the maimed ape have...

*(*RONNIE *screams, possessed, falls to floor and is caught by* JOCKEY. *She begins to speak in tongues. She raises, still speaking in tongues and moves in a rhythmic dance.)*

OX TAIL: ...her say.

EL TORO: *(As* MINISTER *directs energy toward* CYNTHIA*)* Take the plunge...

*(*CYNTHIA *screams, possessed, falls and is caught by* KATHLEEN. *She begins to speak in tongues, rises and moves in a rhythmic dance.)*

EL TORO: ...and speak in tongues.
Mother song
And father sound.

(As the song Speak in Tongues *comes to an end,* OTHER MEMBERS *of the group become obsessed, fall to the floor and speak in tongues. As the speaking goes on, they let their tongues direct the movement of their bodies until they are lifted off the floor and go into rhythmic dance.* PARISHIONERS *who speak in tongues during the song keep the volume down, allowing it to rise when the singers are silent.* KATHLEEN *and* JOCKEY *[still as* PARISHONERS*] scream, possessed. Then they begin to speak in tongues and rhythmically move in dance. With* PARISHIONERS *speaking in tongues,* OX TAIL *as* MINISTER ONE *and* EL TORO *as* MINISTER TWO *come to the center and pray.)*

MINISTER ONE: I pray to the Lord with all my heart and soul to give me the grace and understanding to interpret the message you are sending here. Especially for all the souls gathered here today in your name. Hallelujah, praise the Lord. The Power is moving. The Power is speaking.

(She is drawn to CYNTHIA, *who is speaking in tongues, and lays her hands on her.)*

MINISTER ONE: Praise the Lord. Hallelujah. This sweet soul saying...

*(*CYNTHIA *becomes silent as her speaking in tongues is translated by the* MINISTER.*)*

MINISTER ONE: "Bask in the light and believe, sister and believe, brothers. The Lord is here—we are blessed and loved if we will only open up our hearts." Do you believe? I believe! Praise the Lord!

*(*CYNTHIA *continues to move rhythmically in celebration. She no longer speaks in tongues.)*

MINISTER TWO: Praise the Lord!

(Moves to RONNIE *who is speaking in tongues, lays hands on her)*

MINISTER TWO: And this dear child of God, this believer is saying to us brothers and sisters... What?

(Pulls Tongues *speech from* RONNIE *and translates—*RONNIE *is silenced.)*

MINISTER TWO: ..."This container is too small..." *(Puzzles over this for a moment, then bows head, smiles and looks up)* Thank you, Lord.

RONNIE: *(Dancing rhythmically in celebration)* Thank you, Jesus.

MINISTER ONE: Praise the Lord, Hallelujah! God is sending me the ability to translate this divine message into English.

MINISTER TWO: The message is coming now, through this instrument who speaks in tongues—

MINISTER ONE: —this instrument created in God's image.

*(*MINISTERS ONE *and* TWO *lay hands on* KATHLEEN *and* JOCKEY *who are still speaking in tongues. Looking up into the light, they begin to translate—at first haltingly, then building with full confidence.* JOCKEY *and* KATHLEEN *stop speaking as their tongues are translated.)*

MINISTER TWO: The answer to the question, "Where are the women inventors and artists of the past?" is....

(The MINISTERS *move to the center of the playing area, stand back to back and move in a circle. Each revelation comes to them like a bolt of lightning.)*

MINISTER ONE: They were in the kitchen inventing corn bread.

MINISTER TWO: They were in the kitchen inventing chili.

MINISTER ONE: They were in the kitchen inventing granola.

MINISTER TWO: They were in the kitchen inventing salad.

MINISTER ONE: They were in the kitchen inventing meatloaf.

MINISTER TWO: They were in the kitchen inventing egg foo young.

MINISTER ONE: They were in the kitchen inventing knishes.

MINISTER TWO: They were in the kitchen inventing the hot dog.

MINISTER ONE: They were in the kitchen inventing spaghetti.

MINISTER TWO: They were in the kitchen inventing pancakes.

MINISTER ONE: They were in the kitchen inventing butter.

MINISTER TWO: They were in the kitchen inventing fire.

MINISTER ONE: They were in the bedroom inventing quilts.

MINISTER TWO: They were in the bathroom inventing perfume.

MINISTER ONE: They were in the bathroom inventing soap.

MINISTER TWO: They were in the bathroom inventing the bath.

MINISTER ONE: They were in the sewing room inventing clothes.

MINISTER TWO: They were in the earth inventing farming.

MINISTER ONE: They were in the woods inventing dancing.

MINISTER ONE: They were by the waterfall inventing singing.

(Both MINISTERS *remove their hats.)*

MINISTER ONE: *(As* OX TAIL, *her prisoner self)* They were in your arms—inventing loving.

(All PARISHIONERS *take off their hats. A very, very brief smile to audience. Then all run to the television room area in front of cells and sit down to watch T V. Throughout this scene they rearrange and knock each other around to get the best view of the T V.* KATHLEEN *is in her cell, separated from the rest, but also watches the T V.)*

CHAMP: I'm sick of Sesame Street!

EL TORO: The Warden loves it.

KATHLEEN: Change the channel.

JOCKEY: I wanna see....

RONNIE: *(Covering* JOCKEY*'s mouth)* Close your mouth and maybe you can.

JOCKEY: Your mother sucks worms.

RONNIE: That's what yer Daddy's got fer a dick.

JOCKEY: I'm gonna tie you to the wall and you got to watch Sesame Street forever.

RONNIE: I'd rather watch that than your ugly mug.

CHAMP: Be cool. Be cool.

EL TORO: Mrs Johnson's gonna put you in the hole.

RONNIE: Where you was born.

JOCKEY: Right behind you. You was born out of a behind.

RONNIE: Shithead.

JOCKEY: You look like the garbage can on the T V show.

RONNIE: Lame, you're too dumb to fight with.

JOCKEY: I get my ideas from the cookie monster.

KATHLEEN: The Munsters have returned.

EL TORO: Morticia, let's start burning the bodies.

CHAMP: Here, light 'em with vampire piss—it works faster than lighter fluid.

KATHLEEN: Shut up, all of you—I'm trying to learn to spell.

RONNIE: The hell with you. *(Singing)* "Take me away baby, baby. Come closer to me and I'll give you my secret key."

CHAMP: Turn up the show and drown out that cat in heat.

*(*CYNTHIA *and* EL TORO *transform into* MATRON ONE *and* MATRON TWO. *They put on coats by the cells and walk toward the Warden's area, keeping a careful eye on members of the audience, nodding at someone they know, looking for contraband, stopping any trouble they see. When they reach the net, they keep watch, then do the following as a "conductor" exercise.)*

MATRON ONE: *(As they watch* OX TAIL*)* She's so cool all the time.

MATRON TWO: Is she real or acting?

MATRON ONE: Anyone who winds up here and acts as sweet as that has got to be acting.

MATRON TWO: She'll do easy time then.

MATRON ONE: Not if I get to her.

MATRON TWO: You're taking this job too serious.

MATRON ONE: What else is there to do? God put me on this earth for a reason. I'm a good wife. I try and pray to be a good mother, and if I can help one other person, then my life will be worthwhile.

MATRON TWO: She's so sweet. Are you sure it's an act?

MATRON ONE: The Warden said if we can get her angry and fighting, then sure as shootin' we can "get through" and help her straighten out.

MATRON TWO: But it takes so much energy to deal with them when they fight back.

MATRON ONE: You're a Christian, aren't you?

MATRON TWO: Of course I'm a Christian!

MATRON ONE: Then take pity on that poor girl, and do what you have to do to get her to see the light.

MATRON TWO: I admire you—I really, really do. I try hard to be a good Christian, but I'm not clear all the time in my mind, just what's the right way to go about....

MATRON ONE: I never have any doubt about what is right and what is wrong. I never have had—my Daddy and Mama taught me that real early.

(They take one last look at the yard, then march back to the cells, keeping their eyes on both sides of the audience as they go. MATRON TWO *transforms back into* EL TORO. CYNTHIA *remains* MATRON ONE *and rattles chain on cells, signaling the women to come down into the yard for recreation.* PRISONERS *wear gym shorts and "Coyote" [the prostitutes' union] T-shirts. Some are doing calisthenics, some basketball, jump rope, run in place, etc. Cell lights and twinkle lights come up abruptly on* RONNIE*'s cell.)*

RONNIE: *(Very "spaced out")* I got busted last summer in Colorado Springs. What a lousy jail. All we got to eat twice a day was cold oatmeal, nothin' to put on it, and coffee made o' sewer water. They gave us Top tobacco to smoke. Stale—it was so stale, I like to set my eyebrows on fire ev'r' time I lit up. *Whoooooooosh* like the Fourth O' July. Went to the hospital with second-degree burns on my eyelids. No shit. No shit! They finally felt so bad about it they let me out for only six bucks. So I high-tailed it for Boulder. There I spent three beautiful days with this spaced-out dude in a bare van. There was nothing in this big Dodge van but, get this, man—nothing in it but this giant black leather rocking chair. This spaced-out dude, he had this chair built just for him for tripping. He loved that chair so much he took it on vacation with him. Hooked this fucking chair right up to the generator, and man, he'd sit in it, drop P C P, M B D, acid, and half my thorazines, and he'd rock himself into ecstatic oblivion. You know what he had built into the seat of his chair?—vibrator, man. *(Pause)* Far out!

(Lights come down on RONNIE, *up on* EL TORO, *who stands behind the net—she is high on pills.)*

EL TORO: Hi, my name's Toro. Man, I'm clean, no shit. Wanna see my arms? Look. *(Rolls up sleeves)* See there—you can't see no tracks there. I quit the needle. I quit it. I quit the needle and I cut my hair. See how clean and neat I look, just like they want me. Never found my real mother till I was sixteen. Ain't that right, Champ?

CHAMP: *(Doing calisthenics in the yard)* That's right, Toro.

EL TORO: This here is my friend Champ. We was together in reform school. We was there four or five years. Hell, Champ was born there—right, Champ? We been in forever. We know the score—right, Champ?

CHAMP: Right.

EL TORO: *(Rolls up sleeves again)* See them arms? When I first kissed my husband I fell right in love with him. Just like that, my knees went just like this. *(Wiggles knees, "makes like" to faint)* I went home and told my Mom—I hadn't known my Mom too long at the time—it took me so fuckin' long to find her—but I told her, I'm gonna marry that guy, and sure enough, four weeks later we was married, and four weeks after that I started on the needle. But then he ratted on me, so I shot him. You seen the bullet holes, didn't you Champ?

CHAMP: I seen 'em, Toro.

(After her speech, RONNIE *comes down from her cell, puts on a guard coat and transforms into a* MATRON. *She doesn't hear* EL TORO, *who's in another part of the building. She signals to other prisoners that recreation is over and they must scrub the floor. She throws scrub brushes to them.)*

EL TORO: Sure enough. But we got lucky and we're still in love. Then we got busted together for dealing—he's in prison at the men's penal complex.

CHAMP: The penis complex.

EL TORO: Right, that's what I got. Anyway, we got lucky and we're still in love, he didn't die, but what a rat he was. Well, I can't help it—I did fall in love with him, just like lightning striking... that's the way it was.

(Lights come down on EL TORO. *Focus shifts to the floor where the* PRISONERS *are scrubbing, covering sections of the floor in pairs:* OX TAIL *and* CHAMP, CYNTHIA *and* EL TORO *[who has come down and joined her],* JOCKEY *and* KATHLEEN.*)*

MATRON: *(Talks down to prisoners)* You ladies should be down like that on your knees three times a day, thanking the good Lord you were born in this time, in this country.

(MATRON's attention shifts, with crowlike eyes, to the audience—eyes darting from one person to another each time the PRISONERS sing. PRISONERS sing to each other, then tenderly caress, cuddle and make love to each other, always keeping an eye on the matron to be sure that her eyes are elsewhere. When the MATRON speaks, the WOMEN begin furiously scrubbing.)

OX TAIL: *(Sings to CHAMP)*
You may put your head down,
You may sink into the pillows of love.

JOCKEY: *(Sings to KATHLEEN)*
You may put your hand down,
You may unclench your fist,
You may unlock your joints.

(PRISONERS separate and go back to fierce scrubbing when they hear the MATRON say:)

MATRON: Before this great country was made into a country, you, Jockey, you, Ox Tail, and you, Champ, would 'a been hanged. Just like that. No ifs ands or buts. Taken out and hanged by your neck until you were dead... for stealing, for picking pockets. No pleading, no mercy—out! Hanged!

(MATRON changes focus to the audience, looking for contraband, sudden movements, anything suspicious. PRISONERS sing and tenderly caress one another, MATRON still oblivious.)

CYNTHIA: *(Sings to EL TORO)*
You may put your head down,
You my sink into the pillows of love.

KATHLEEN *(Sings to JOCKEY)*/EL TORO *(Sings to CYNTHIA)*/
CHAMP: *(Sings to OX TAIL)*
You may put your belly down.
The Lord will provide.
There is no need to strive
For food or drink.

MATRON: *(PRISONERS separate and scrub)* For a misdemeanor they'd cut off your hands. For adultery, a brand on your forehead—a big brand right here in the middle of your forehead—and without a valium yet.

(PRISONERS join hands, dance in a circle around the MATRON, who doesn't see them because she's watching the audience.)

PRISONERS: *(Sing)* Music will fill
All the empty spaces.

You may lay away need,
Dissolve desire.

(They spin out, reform with same partners, go to three separate areas of the floor.)

OX TAIL, JOCKEY & CYNTHIA: *(Sing)* Stay a while.

CHAMP, KATHLEEN & EL TORO: *(Sing)* Stay a while.

KATHLEEN & JOCKEY: *(Sing in center section)*
Hello eye—may I have the next dance?
Hello lips—be still now.

*(*PRISONERS *scrub.)*

MATRON: You don't know how lucky you are, ladies. How'd you like that, El Toro—get those pretty hands of yours cut off, for bad checks—both of them? How'd you like that?

JOCKEY: I'd like it, because then I'd be done with you!

*(*MATRON *turns quickly, signals her to get back to work)*

EL TORO: *(Sings)* Your heart beats out our trance.

CHAMP: *(Sings)* Hello tongue—this trip has just begun.

ALL PRISONERS & MATRON: *(Sing)* This is the place
Where light is feed.
The Lord will provide.
I've got what you need.
You may hide your sweet,
Burdened head
In this dancing bed.

(The PRISONERS *continue scrubbing.* EL TORO *quickly and cautiously scrubs toward* JOCKEY, *stares at her, smiles, tries to catch her eye, clears her throat, or lets her brush get away from her so that they somehow touch or get very close.)*

EL TORO: *(Very quietly)* I know who you are.

*(*JOCKEY *freezes)*

EL TORO: Don't worry. Lotsa people love you....

*(*JOCKEY *deliberately scrubs away from her)*

EL TORO: Really, don't worry. I'm not gonna blow yer cover.

(They freeze. Lights come down slowly.)

END OF ACT ONE

ACT TWO

(More new women prisoners are being admitted. They enter in darkness and take their places behind the net. As the lights come up, they project images of " looking for a way out". The group stops and listens, moves together, stops together. They range in age from seventeen to sixty. Those who've never been to prison before might keep their eyes downcast [they try to minimize their presence]. The political prisoners hold themselves erect and proud. They size up the situation and try to make contact with those with whom they can establish "lines" of sympathy. "Repeaters" are greeted like alums returning to an old school, by both inmates and guards with hearty recognition. CHAMP *is not among the prisoners—she enters the yard as* MATRON.*)*

MATRON: Take a chair, ladies. When your name is called, come forward to claim your property and valuables—and, I repeat—check the list. Bessie Mayo.

KATHLEEN: *(Transformed into* BETSY*)* That's Betsy!

MATRON: The name on the official Department list is Bessie, so that's your name.

BETSY: They wrote it down wrong.

MATRON: *(Flat tone, calling out again)* Bessie Mayo.

BETSY: My name is Betsy. I won't be called a name not my own.

MATRON: You are in prison. You have no more rights. You gave up your rights when you committed the crime that sent you here. The name on my list, written here by the Authorities, is Bessie Mayo.

BETSY: Betsy!

MATRON: Any more outbursts and you'll be taken to Adjustment.

EL TORO: Shut up, honey, and do like she says, or they throw you in the hole.

BETSY: I protest this deliberate dehumanizing process. You are beginning by taking away my own name. Well, it's going to stop right here, because I will not tolerate...

MATRON: Oh, swell, we got a Commie in this bunch. Take her away.

*(*BETSY *backs away from the net. The following roll call may be added to or changed at any given performance to include some names of audience members or newsworthy people. The actors transform to these different personalities. We used a*

set order in which the actors always responded: (1) EL TORO *(2)* JOCKEY *(3)*RONNIE, *etc.)*

MATRON: Adelle Novas.

ADELLE: Here.

MATRON: Marijane Scoppetone.

MARIJANE: Here.

MATRON: Maimie Eisenhower.

MAIMIE: Here.

MATRON: Ida Lupino.

IDA: Here.

MATRON: Happy Ford.

HAPPY: Here.

*(*PRISONERS *begin to come out from behind the net and line up in front of it.)*

MATRON: Betty Rockefeller.

BETTY: Here.

MATRON: Louise Lasser.

LOUISE: Here.

MATRON: Tricia DietRite.

TRICIA: Here.

MATRON: Amy Carter.

AMY: Here.

MATRON: Marlena Dexadrine.

MARLENE: Here.

*(*MATRON *crosses to net, turns, removes her jacket and becomes a* PRISONER. *She joins the others, who are acting out their fantasies of what they'll do and be when they get out. They dream of being safe-crackers, tennis champs, typists, etc.)*

JOCKEY: *(Sings, as others continue acting out their fantasies)*
When I get out of here
I'm gonna make so much money
I'll never have any fear. *(Runs onto floor and sits)*

RONNIE: *(Sings)* When I get out of here...

(Punches others, who fall like dominoes)

RONNIE: I'm gonna dress so sharp *(Jives on floor)* And keep my eyes piercing clear.

(OX TAIL *and* CYNTHIA *pick up* JOCKEY, EL TORO *picks up* RONNIE, *both groups perform flying images.* CHAMP *and* KATHLEEN *perform images singly.)*

RONNIE: I'll buy me a Lear jet
And you can bet—

ALL: I'm gonna fly, I'm gonna fly.

RONNIE: I'm gonna go go go go go go go go go go! *(Flying image ends.)*

KATHLEEN: *(Sings, with others keeping time from floor)*
When I get out of here
I'll get me so much bread
They'll think I invented dough

ALL: *(Sing)* I'll jet by so high you won't see me go,
I'll jet by so high you won't see me go,
I'll jet by so high you won't see me go!
I'll be so high,
I'll be so high,
You won't see me go go go go go go go go go go!

(JOCKEY, OX TAIL *and* KATHLEEN *transform into* MATRON ONE, MATRON TWO *and* MATRON THREE. MATRON ONE *begins to harass a* PRISONER *and push her around for no visible reason. [She may not have scrubbed floor properly, or she may have been seen "with" another prisoner.]* MATRONS TWO *and* THREE *intervene, causing* MATRON ONE *to let* PRISONER *go, then they bring* MATRON ONE *with them to the* WARDEN'*s area where all three keep watch on the yard.)*

MATRON ONE: I did what I had to do.

MATRON TWO: You kept control.

MATRON THREE: Best of all, you kept control of *yourself.*

MATRON ONE: I'm a human being—I have feelings just like anybody else.

MATRON TWO: You did right.

MATRON THREE: Every time something like that's happened, it's always from nerves.

MATRON TWO: It's usually always nerves.

MATRON THREE: These girls all got too many nerves. 'Member one from Birmingham, was wound up all the time? Her eyes just glowed.

MATRON TWO: I remember her—all the girls had crushes on her.

MATRON THREE: Like to scratch each other's eyes out.

MATRON TWO: They was always searching her cell and her body.

MATRON THREE: The Warden was sure she was on something.

MATRON TWO: It was just nerves, just nerves that made her eyes glow like that—but let me tell you, no one wanted to turn their backs on her.

MATRON ONE: Should I call?

MATRON TWO: Honey, it isn't your fault. She'll pull through.

MATRON ONE: I swear I thought she'd stuffed a pillow in her stomach, just to bug me. It didn't look natural the way her belly was spread out like that. She was flat as a board at morning count.

MATRON THREE: Some of these women is just demons—they can think their way into anything. She got herself all worked up just because her mother died. She'll be okay in the morning, mark my words.

MATRON ONE: I didn't hit her. I'm not the type. I'd never lose control like that.

(During the following "nodding" lines, the actors continue the nodding action as an "emblem" throughout the speech.)

MATRON TWO: I was there. You just pushed on her belly to see if it was a pillow.

MATRON ONE: *(Nods)* That's right. That's all I did.

MATRON THREE: *(Nods)* I can just hear the troublemakers now.

MATRON ONE: *(Nods)* That Squaw was standing just round the corner. She's telling the whole population I hit her in the stomach and that's why she swelled up. *(Nodding stops)*

MATRON THREE: In the old days they'd have thrown her in the hole 'til she got over agitating. They kept an Indian in there once til she went blind—didn't give nobody any trouble after that, you can bet your boots.

MATRON ONE: It's not my fault they won't give her leave to go to the funeral. I don't make the rules.

MATRON TWO: Just grief made her belly act like that. My God, she looked eight months pregnant.

MATRON THREE: She was flat as a board this morning.

MATRON TWO: It's just nerves, honey. You did your job, and you kept yourself in control in front of the rest of them. That's what you're supposed to do and that's what you're paid to do.

MATRON ONE: If we took them in our arms every time they got bad news from home, the whole place would fall apart.

MATRON THREE: You can bet your boots.

MATRON TWO: You can say that again.

(They stand at attention, remove their uniform jackets and transform back into PRISONERS. *All* PRISONERS *now "walk" back and forth from the net to their cells. Some interact non-verbally asking for tenderness, others maintain solitude, some look for comfort, a fight, etc. Those they "ask" comply or resist, but some sort of*

contact is made. This contact is always broken when they hear something, think a guard is approaching or are "caught in the act" and each continues walking alone until a new contact is made. The walking continues until RONNIE *and* EL TORO *are in their cells—then the others move quickly to theirs.* CHAMP *and* KATHLEEN *share the same cell.* CHAMP *rubs* KATHLEEN*'s back.)*

EL TORO: *(To* RONNIE *who's transformed into an older woman)* What are you in for?

RONNIE: *(As older woman)* Life.

EL TORO: I mean...charge...?

RONNIE: *(Looks at her a moment)* Oh yeah...murder.

(They freeze. So do OX TAIL, JOCKEY *and* CYNTHIA *who've been listening. Focus shifts to* KATHLEEN *and* CHAMP.*)*

CHAMP: What are you in for?

KATHLEEN: Bum rap.

CHAMP: Aren't we all?

KATHLEEN: I didn't do anything.

CHAMP: But they caught you at it.

KATHLEEN: I was in the wrong place...

CHAMP: ...at the wrong time...

KATHLEEN: Yeah...

(They freeze. Focus shifts to RONNIE, EL TORO *and* JOCKEY.*)*

EL TORO: Wow.

JOCKEY: When.

RONNIE: When what?

OX TAIL: When'd ya do it?

RONNIE: Many lives ago.

JOCKEY: Who was it?

RONNIE: A husband of that period.

OX TAIL: Did you do it?

RONNIE: I didn't, but it doesn't matter. I did it a lot in my head, before and since.

(They freeze. Focus shifts to KATHLEEN *and* CHAMP.*)*

CHAMP: I been watching you.

KATHLEEN: Oh?

CHAMP: Been watching you eat.

KATHLEEN: Yeah?

CHAMP: I like to watch your mouth.

*(*KATHLEEN *laughs.* CHAMP *stops rubbing)*

CHAMP: You got family?

KATHLEEN: I guess.

CHAMP: *(Pushes her)* Do ya or don't ya?

KATHLEEN: *(Confused)* They're still there, I guess.

CHAMP: *(Starts to get rougher)* Where?

KATHLEEN: *(Moves away)* South Dakota.

CHAMP: *(Shakes* KATHLEEN*)* How long since you were home?

KATHLEEN: *(Presses herself)* Left at fifteen.

CHAMP: *(Pins her up against wall)* Didn't they try to stop you?

KATHLEEN: *(Stands up to* CHAMP*)* I didn't give 'em a chance. I ironed all my Dad's shirts and I left.

CHAMP: *(This was the response she wanted—it was a game.)* Far out...I really like the look of you.

KATHLEEN: *(Still confused)* Thanks.

(They freeze. Focus shifts to RONNIE *and the others.)*

EL TORO: How long you been in the joint?

RONNIE: Sixteen years here. Four in the maximum facility. Eighteen months before that in the county jail. That was the pits. The others were better, but *(Reaches over to stroke* JOCKEY*)* this one's best of all.

JOCKEY: But you shoulda been paroled by now.

RONNIE: They've been trying to get me out of here all right.

OX TAIL: Were you given a fair hearing?

RONNIE: They granted parole, three times now, but I refused it.

EL TORO: Why? Why? Why? I...I want outa here so bad I....

RONNIE: I'm innocent.

JOCKEY: No shit.

RONNIE: Besides, it's safer here than on the streets or even in my own home.

JOCKEY: But it's so boring.

(All fall into images of enormous boredom for a beat. They change into other images of boredom in time with the musical introduction. They leave their cells and create

one big "bored" image in front of the cells. Their action during this "scat" song is to find relief from the boredom of prison—they act out fantasies of what they'd like to do if free. They start in front of the cells and move, singing and dancing, across the whole yard.)

EL TORO, CHAMP & OX TAIL: *(Sing)*	JOCKEY & KATHLEEN: *(Sing)*	RONNIE: *(Sings)*
I'm bored		
	I'm bored	
		I'm bored
I'm sick		
And tired		
I'm sick and		
Tired		
Of being		
Sick		
And tired.		
I'm sick and		
Tired of		
Being sick		
And tired.	Bored	Bored.
I'm so bored		
	Sick!	I'm sick
Sick!		And tired
		I'm tired of
		Bein'
Tired!	Tired!	Tired of bein'
		Sick,
		Tired of bein'
Bored!	Bored!	Sick and tired,
		Tired of bein'
	My	Sick and tired.
	Ass is bored	
	Off.	
That's the problem		My ass is bored off.
	The main problem	
Love!	Is—	No stimulation
No stimulation,	No stimulation,	No stimulation.
No stimulation,	No stimulation,	
No stimulation.	Never mind.	Never mind.
	Satisfaction	Satisfaction.
	I'll take	I'll take satisfaction
Is there a mind	Stimulation	
Left to rot?		Satisfaction.
Stimulate,	You don't need	Stimulate,
Stimulate	No mind if you got	Stimulate,

Stimulate the
Soul inmate.

I'll go to the hole.

But
Then they'll put us
In separate holes.
I'm ready, I'm
Ready, oh yes,
I'm ready!
Stimulate this
Little old inmate
Flash me a scratch,
Flash me a be-bop
Up the side of
My head
Flash me a punch
Flash me a snatch.

I need it!
Anything!
One more time to
Walk with a flash
On my patch,
One more time to
Roll out to freedom
One more time to
Walk in Jerusalem
One more time,
One more time to
Feel the—

And the sun on my arms
One more time,
One more time,

Soul.

Stimulate,
Stimulate.
I'll go with you.

But
Think of the fun
We'll have getting
There.
Oh please let
Me out of here!

Oh, I'm ready!
Oh, I'm ready!
to be
An eternal incarcerate
Just one more
Time, get me
flashing,—
Just one more time

Oh oh, Stroke my soul

Fight with me baby.

But
Think of the fun
We'll have getting
There.
Stimulate this
Little old inmate
Flash me a scratch,
Flash me a be-bop
Up the side of
My head
Flash me a punch.
Flash me a snatch.
Flash!

Flash! Flash!
One more time to
Walk with a flash
On my patch
One more time to
Roll out to freedom
One more time to
Feel the flash of cash,
One more time,
One more time to
Feel the
Cold on my nose.

One more time,
One more time,

Make me happy to be
Walking,
Be happy to be walking,
Be happy to be walking.
Flash!
I got the
Fascination
With stimulation.
Flash me a scratch.
I got the fascination
With the stimulation.
Flash me a patch.
I got the
Fascination with the
Stimulation,
Fascination with the
Stimulation.
One more time.
One more time.

Flash me a scratch,	Oh, I'm ready,	Flash me a scratch,
Flash me a be-bop,	Oh, I'm ready,	Flash me a be-bop
Up the side		Up the side
Of my head,	To be	Of my head,
Flash me a punch,	An eternal	Flash me a punch,
Flash me a snatch.	Incarcer-	Flash me a snatch,
	ate.	Flash!
I need it!		
Anything!	Just one more	Flash! Flash!
One more time	Time to get me flashing,	One more time,
To walk with a	Just one more time	Walk with a
Flash on my patch.		Flash on my patch.
One more time to	Make me happy to be	One more time to
	Walking	
Roll out to freedom	Be happy to be walking,	Roll out to freedom
One more time to	Be happy to be walking	One more time to
Walk in Jerusalem.	Flash! I got the	Feel the flash of cash
One more time,	Fascination with the	One more time,
	Stimulation.	
One more time	Flash me a scratch	One more time
To feel the—		To feel the
	I got the	Cold on my nose.
And the sun on	Fascination with the	
My arms	Stimulation.	
One more time	Flash me a scratch.	One more time,
To walk in	I got the	Walk in

Jerusalem	Fascination with the Stimulation.	Jerusalem
Holding hands With my love One more time, One more time.	Fascination With the stimulation. One more time, One more time.	Holding hands With my love. One more time, One more time.

(All hold. RONNIE *turns to the others, who feel good having played out their fantasies. They sit around. The following scene is a continuation of the scene before the song.)*

RONNIE: Look inside. It isn't boring in here. *(Taps her head)* Nehru wrote twenty-six books in jail. Elizabeth Gurley Flynn wrote a damn good one, too.

EL TORO: Ney—who?

JOCKEY: Are you writing?

RONNIE: Takes too much time away from listening.

JOCKEY: Come again?

RONNIE: *(Grabs* JOCKEY *intimately and slightly rough)* I'd he happy to teach you, if you truly want to learn. I'm a Leo and have dominion over children. I haven't time for kidding or mockery. I'm interested in beauty. *(Looks around, chooses* CYNTHIA, *mainly as a lesson for* JOCKEY*)* I need clear eyes to look into, and beautiful skin to keep me giving. *(To* JOCKEY*)* If you change your dietary habits to improve your looks, I'll consider sharing some discoveries with you. *(Slaps* JOCKEY *playfully but firmly)* If you want to know—really "know" demonstrate this to me by getting hold of yourself and improving your health habits. *(To* KATHLEEN*)* And you, there, you're too short. Hold your torso up, get your head out of your neck. *(Turns and walks toward the cells)*

CHAMP: Christ, she's a Leo, all right.

EL TORO: I'm sorry I talked to her.

KATHLEEN: Do you think she did it?

EL TORO: Who cares?

JOCKEY: *(Dreamily looking after her)* I'm in love.

(Others laugh, call her a masochist, etc.)

(At O M T the following scene was played with physical action juxtaposed to the lines: before saying a line, the actor selects a physical contact activity and imposes it on another. The one "imposed on" has to decide to go along with it or resist. The one "imposing her will" continues the activity until replaced by a stronger will. The action imposed should have no logical connection with the line said. A different will [intention] is imposed with each line.)

*(*KATHLEEN *and* CHAMP *come up behind* JOCKEY*, bring her to the middle of the prison yard.)*

KATHLEEN: What are they putting in our food?

CHAMP: What food?

JOCKEY: That ain't no food, man—where I come from the roaches turn their noses up at it.

KATHLEEN: I'm so tired all the time.

JOCKEY: They mean for us to be.

CHAMP: That's right—they mean for us to be, so's we can't be mean.

JOCKEY: And our pee turns green.

CHAMP: Only thing to do is to quit.

KATHLEEN: I've quit. I can't hold out. I don't want to get out of bed.

CHAMP: You got to quit eating the food.

JOCKEY: They got it all drugged up.

CHAMP: They throwed us in here for drugs, and they's using more on us than the Mafia ever brought across the border.

JOCKEY: You notice Witch-Freak don't talk no more.

CHAMP: I noticed.

KATHLEEN: What'd they do to her?

JOCKEY: They hit her with eight Thorazine. Everytime she looks like she's gonna say somethin', they give her another.

KATHLEEN: I had a Thorazine once, and I didn't wake up for thirty-six hours.

CHAMP: We all got different chemistry. You's a cheap date, baby.

(All laugh.)

KATHLEEN: I don't have the strength to write a letter.

CHAMP: You got a lover on the streets?

KATHLEEN: Yeah, yeah. I know where she is, too.

CHAMP: Do she know where you is?

*(*JOCKEY *and* CHAMP *look at each other. A slight nod passes between them.)*

JOCKEY: She on your list to get mail?

KATHLEEN: I wouldn't do that. I don't want them to know about her.

CHAMP: Where'd you meet? I love love stories.

KATHLEEN: Church picnic.

CHAMP & JOCKEY: *(Laughing)* Oh yeah? Oh yeah? O Wow! What a scene!

KATHLEEN: Well it was. She was from another state. She had a special way of talking. It sounded like singing—but I know she was talking straight to me.

JOCKEY: You got religion?

KATHLEEN: She's my God now—I know no other. It was in the middle of the song I was singing. She was standing beside me, I felt her looking at me, and my voice grew stronger. Then I thought I was getting taller—I looked down at my feet, but I got dizzy. All the people in the audience were looking up at me and they smiled. I turned my head just a bit in the middle of a note, and I caught this blaze in her eyes and I got even stronger. My voice went out to the trees. I handed her the mike. I didn't need it to reach the people. She turned off the mike and held my hand. I sang for an hour, then she helped me from the stage. We went straight to my tent.

JOCKEY: Did you make love?

KATHLEEN: We didn't have to. She was still holding my hand. The light in her eyes nearly blinded me. They were the clearest, lightest blue I've ever seen. Whenever I looked directly at her the heavens opened up behind her head, and rays came from her body-rays that held me up, rays that drew me to her. She didn't know she had these rays.... They were invisible. I could feel them as sure as I can feel this floor. l knew I could never fall again. Knew I would never fall. All I would have to do is think about her eyes, and they would always see me—and see her body and she would always hold me.

CHAMP: And that's all you did?

JOCKEY: You didn't make out?

KATHLEEN: Leave me alone. I can't get it together.

JOCKEY: You should get more protein, girl.

KATHLEEN: I thought you said we should quit eating.

JOCKEY: Well, we should probably try it and get our systems cleaned out. But I personally don't think you're strong enough.

(They freeze in the last "will imposed" and begin a section of "walks." JOCKEY *crosses to* OX TAIL*'s cell, where twinkle lights blink on.)*

OX TAIL: I made a big mistake.

JOCKEY: *(Joins her in cell)* I thought you were gonna play the field from now on.

OX TAIL: I'm stuck.

CHAMP: Do you realize how many times you've been in love in the last two years?

OX TAIL: The more it happens, the harder it hits. I thought you got used to stuff like this.

RONNIE: *(Struts through prison yard to* OX TAIL*'s cell)* The cool like me, we never fall. We let them fall for us. Now me, I got two women working for my validation. Women got to be trained. Can't let them get the upper hand. Even the screws know that. They get out of line, you kick their ass—they'll get down on their knees and kiss your foot. I'm fixing to add another wife soon. You watch how I break the new one in. You do what I do, and you won't feel low down and blue no more. You understand?
(Sings) Look around you, hon.
Everywhere y' see
In the prison yard
Or mincing on T V.
You see nothin', hon.
You see nothin', hon.
But a bunch of
Beautiful babes.
Everyone—guarded
By guns.

ALL: *(Sing softly under)* Hi ya, Betty
Hello Nancy.
Come out Barbara.
Come back Marilyn.
I love Lucy,
Ethel too.
Why don't *you*
Run for
President—Rose?

We're all Babes in the Bighouse,
We're all Babes in the Bighouse,
We're all Babes in the Bighouse,
Trained to love the son of a gun!

RONNIE: So-o-o-o-o-o-the
Only the way to go
Is to let nothin' show.
(Others softly repeat "Hello Betty" etc.)
You gotta be cool
If you wanna do
Easy time like me.

ALL: We're all Babes in the Bighouse,
We're all Babes in the Bighouse,
We're all Babes in the Bighouse,
Trained to love the son of a gun!

RONNIE: These women are confused,
Broken and abused,
So how do I show my class—?
I kick 'em in the ass!

ALL: We're all Babes in the Bighouse,
We're all Babes in the Bighouse,
We're all Babes in the Bighouse,
Trained to love the son of a gun!

RONNIE: Follow my simple golden rule.
Show 'em who's boss—
Nobody fools the cool—
Nail her to the cross!

ALL: Babes in the Bighouse,
Babes in the Bighouse,
The bughouse,
The Bighouse—
Hello Babes!
Hello Babes!
(Up you, Mister!
Free my sister!)
We're all Babes in the Bighouse,
Babes! Babes! Babes!

(Lights come up suddenly on the warden's area, in front of the net. EL TORO *has transformed into* GLORIA SWENSON *and is being interrogated by* MATRONS ONE *and* TWO *[*JOCKEY *and* CHAMP*]. All three face the audience with the* MATRONS standing directly behind GLORIA.*)*

MATRON ONE: At 0-six hundred hours, Gloria Swenson, you were reported by Officer McClannahan on June twelfth *(You may substitute a date closer to performance date)* to be seen in a passionate embrace in the shower with Mary Lou Wiseman. We have rules here, Gloria. This is a very serious offense. Do you have anything to say?

GLORIA: I need another shower.

MATRON TWO: Insolence is also against the rules.

MATRON ONE: Do you wish to compound the charge against you?

GLORIA: I really do need a shower. I haven't been allowed a shower in more than a week.

MATRON TWO: Why not?

GLORIA: Officer McClannahan took my shower privileges away for talking too loud at dinner.

MATRON ONE: You were identified by Officer McClannahan to be in the shower with Mary Lou Wiesman. Is that true?

GLORIA: To quote our beloved ex-President, "I can't recall."

MATRON TWO: *(Snaps* GLORIA'*s head around to look her in the eyes)* President who?

MATRON ONE: *(Gives* MATRON TWO *a signal to release* GLORIA, *then smiles and continues in her own style)* Are you a member of that secret cult?

GLORIA: Yes.

MATRON ONE: *(As if she's forgotten)* What's the name of it?

GLORIA: *(Sotto voce)* Jeffersonian Democracy.

MATRON TWO: *(Excited—snaps* GLORIA'*s head around again)* What?

GLORIA: Jefferson—...

*(*MATRON ONE *more aggressively signals* MATRON TWO *to leave the interrogation to her.)*

MATRON ONE: *(Sizing up* GLORIA'*s "insolence" she holds her around the shoulders)* Looooooooook, Gloria, we're here to help you. Are you going to cooperate and give your side of the story? Or do we accept Officer McClannahan's report and punish you accordingly?

GLORIA: Officer McClannahan lied.

MATRON ONE: Why would Officer McClannahan lie?

GLORIA: *(Animated)* I don't know. But I do need a shower. Here— *(Lifts her arms)* —smell me.

*(*MATRONS *move to the right.* MATRON ONE *kneels,* MATRON TWO *places her chin on* MATRON ONE'*s head. They drop their jaws, mouths hanging "dumb" in a "helplessness" image, then take the line from this position.)*

MATRONS: That is not ladylike behavior. *(They repeat the image.)*

GLORIA: Ladies take showers twice a day. You only let me have a shower once a week. I can't stand my own smell.

MATRON ONE: *(Moving back to her position behind* GLORIA*)* When did you stop engaging in homosexual behavior with Mary Lou Wiseman?

GLORIA: When I stopped beating my husband.

MATRON TWO: *(Pauses—turns* GLORIA'*s head, looks into her eyes)* Look, Gloria, we do not appreciate these smart remarks. It's going to have to be entered on your record. Is this the sort of record you want to go before your parole board?

GLORIA: No ma'am.

*(*MATRON ONE *gives* MATRON TWO *a sign that she'll handle it now.)*

MATRON ONE: *(Embracing* GLORIA, *who looks at arms around her and laughs to herself)* All right, we're getting somewhere. Now, we want to help you straighten yourself out and get along here. You want to have a clean record, don't you?

GLORIA: I want to have a clean record and I want to have a clean body.

*(*MATRONS *move to left, repeat "helpless" image in a slightly different combination with* MATRON TWO *squatting,* MATRON ONE *on top. They drop their jaws.)*

MATRONS: Put her in Adjustment until she decides to answer our questions like a rational human being.

(They repeat image, mouths hanging open and maintain this through next speech)

GLORIA: I ain't done anything. You can't put me in the hole for smelling bad. It's your fault. You don't even give hot water. I want some soap. Soap? I haven't been near a shower in more than two weeks. You liars. You ladies. You lady liars. Come out of your closets, you bulldykes, you secret cunt cocksuckers! You're the liars! You're the liars!

MATRON TWO: Take her away.

*(*MATRON TWO *removes her guard coat and becomes* JOCKEY *again.* GLORIA/EL TORO *puts on guard coat and transforms into a* MATRON. RONNIE, *as* MATRON ONE, *watches the audience as she crosses the space, takes a place on the platform in front of the net.* EL TORO, RONNIE *and* CHAMP *impose their wills on one another physically or watch prisoners and audience for trouble as they sing.* JOCKEY, KATHLEEN, OX TAIL *and* CYNTHIA, *in their cells, work on "finding a way out"—they move and step together as they sing.)*

MATRONS: *(Sing)* This is occupied territory.

PRISONERS: *(Sing)* We live in occupied territory.
Are you ready to love
Beyond your fingernail?
There is a vast body to behold—
That body is you.

MATRONS: *(Reaching out to* PRISONERS*)* I implore you to swim into the
Mainstream of your own conscious being,
And live in your whole body, too.
Aren't you cramped there, under that
Damp, dirty nail?

PRISONERS: *(To audience. Describing prison life)*
Expand outward into your fist.
Let your mind exist in
Your chest and rise upward to
The tip of your breast.

ALL: Ahhhhhhhh yes, she feels so good—
And you can feel you, if you only would.

*(*MATRONS *move slowly toward* PRISONERS *with outstretched arms. The* PRISONERS *are suddenly free—this is a fantasy section. The cells open, they crawl out.)*

*(*JOCKEY *and* KATHLEEN *run hand in hand " like youth in the wood," in and out of the line of* MATRONS. OX TAIL *and* CYNTHIA *sing to each other.* MATRONS *still sing to the women.)*

ALL: Let me hold your hand,
And you can live here safely in my land.
I won't give anyone your
Phone number,
But you can call me any time—
Night or day—
And we will—

*(*PRISONERS *embrace,* MATRONS *try to pull them apart—more "imposing of will.")*

ALL: Fling our arms around each other—

(Tug-of war between embracing PRISONERS *and* MATRONS *trying to separate them continues.)*

ALL: And lay and lay land lay
And lay and lay
And lay.

*(*CHAMP *transforms from* MATRON *back to herself and begins scrubbing.* RONNIE *[as* MATRON*] pulls* KATHLEEN *from* JOCKEY*'s arms and throws her to the floor.* KATHLEEN *immediately starts scrubbing toward* CHAMP. RONNIE *and* EL TORO *transform back to prisoners.* PRISONERS *"walk" the yards and corridors as* KATHLEEN *and* CHAMP *scrub.)*

CHAMP: I had a very high standard of living at the Federal Facility. Worked in the laundry and had forty customers a month.

KATHLEEN: How much?

CHAMP: That's a carton of cigarettes per customer.

KATHLEEN: You were rich.

CHAMP: It was real easy time. Some of the women there wanted to look sharp all the time. Know what I mean? And I got paid in cash to starch clothes for the officers.

KATHLEEN: Could you keep it?

*(*RONNIE *is feeling full of herself—she looks around for a conquest, selects* EL TORO, *approaches her and roughly sends her to the cells to get ready, "walks" and watches to make sure that no one saw her speak to* EL TORO.*)*

CHAMP: Naw, it added to my account in the Commissary. But I had anything I wanted there. Anything! I never been so poor in my life as I am here.

KATHLEEN: Me too. There isn't a big enough population to build up a really good bank account.

CHAMP: *(Agreeing)* Tell me about it.

(They continue to scrub. RONNIE *taps* CHAMP *on the back—a signal that* CHAMP *should be lookout while* RONNIE *"tends to some business."* CHAMP *gleefully runs off to do this.* EL TORO *wait anxiously in* RONNIE*'s cell—finally* RONNIE *coolly joins her.)*

RONNIE: *(Not even looking at* EL TORO*—looking out bars)* Lay down on your stomach.

EL TORO: *(Touching* RONNIE*)* Look, I really like you.

RONNIE: *(Shakes her off)* Hurry—we don't have any time.

EL TORO: I love your nose. You got the same perfect nose as Farrah Fawcett *(Or current pop star)*.

RONNIE: *(Forces her down)* No shit! Lay down on this mat.

EL TORO: *(Reaches for her)* I really dig you.

RONNIE: *(Twists her arm)* Then do like I say.

EL TORO: But I want to get to know you. *(Tries to kiss her)*

RONNIE: *(Moves away)* I don't go for mush.

EL TORO: *(Hanging on* RONNIE*)* It's only a little kiss—what you in for?

RONNIE: *(Forces* EL TORO *flat onto mat)* For a while.

EL TORO: You're strong.

RONNIE: *(Over* EL TORO*)* That's right. Turn over.

EL TORO: But I want to look at you. Your face knocks me out.

RONNIE: Take a good look *(Poses)* and turn over.

*(*EL TORO *tries to kiss her some more—*RONNIE *twists her arm 'til she turns over onto her stomach.)*

EL TORO: Hey, at least let me take off my clothes.

RONNIE: *(Leaps onto her)* No time.

EL TORO: Oh, please baby, let's undress if we're gonna make love. I'm crazy about you, baby—you send me around the band. Please. Let's take our clothes off.

RONNIE: *(Putting all her weight on* EL TORO *and beginning to gyrate)* Don't talk. This is the way I do it! I want you to say, "Daddy, my ass is yours."

*(*EL TORO *goes into gales of laugher.* RONNIE *gets off furious, and shakes her.)*

RONNIE: Say it!

EL TORO: *(Laughing some more)* You're a riot!

RONNIE: *(Twisting* EL TORO*'s arm higher, pulling her up so both are kneeling)* I told you not to frustrate your Daddy, little Mama, or I'll have to whip you.

EL TORO: You can't be serious. Hey, I dig you, but this isn't any fun.

RONNIE: *(Pushes her down)* If you dig me, *(Crushes her with her weight)* then you'll please me.

EL TORO: *(Cries out)* You're heavy!

RONNIE: *(Begins to gyrate, pumping on* EL TORO*'s behind)* O Mama, O Mama. You got a beautiful ass. It's all for me, ain't it, Mama? Give me your ass, Little Mama—give your Daddy your great big beautiful ass. Give it to me. *(Pause)* Say it! *(Pause)* Say it! Say, "Daddy, my ass is yours." *(Pause)* Say it!

EL TORO: You're hurting me.

RONNIE: Say it, Mama—tell me. Tell me what you'll give me. Tell me.

EL TORO: Please, let me go. You're crushing me.

RONNIE: *(Bearing down harder, approaching climax)* Say it!

EL TORO: *(Very flat—to get it over with)* Daddy...my ass...is...yours

RONNIE: *(Reaching climax in sighs and spasms, she cries out)* Oh, Mama... *(Whoops, and climbs the bars as high as she can climb)* I love you!

(Lights come up abruptly on the net area. TERESA *[*KATHLEEN*] is "strapped" into the chair, the* DOCTOR *[*JOCKEY*] talking to her. This action began taking place during previous scene in mime on* RONNIE*'s line: "no time,"* JOCKEY *puts on white lab coat and transforms into* DOCTOR*, chooses* CYNTHIA *to help her set up examining room. They cross to the warden's area in front of the net and prepare for a psychiatric examination, setting a large silver armchair with straps on the platform. [In the O M T production, a male mannequin dressed as a "pimp" was set behind the chair, his arms placed on the patient's' shoulders instead of straps.]* KATHLEEN *has transformed into* TERESA—DOCTOR, *[*JOCKEY*] directs* CYNTHIA *to bring* TERESA *into the examining room and after she does, dismisses her back to her cell.)*

DOCTOR: You know why you're here, don't you Teresa? Don't you?

TERESA: I didn't start it.

DOCTOR: But you finished it, didn't you, Teresa? Juanita has a broken jaw, and a broken collarbone. She's the fifth woman you've put in the hospital. You fight too much, Teresa. Women should not fight. It isn't ladylike, is it? You lose your femininity when you fight like a man. Don't you, Teresa?

TERESA: *(Under her breath, but audible)* I could knock you on your ass, too.

DOCTOR: No you can't. You're strapped to the table.

TERESA: I promise I won't fight no more.

DOCTOR: You promised that last time.

TERESA: But I promise. It wasn't my fault. I had to protect myself. Juanita started it.

DOCTOR: Did Caroline start it? *(Mock-throws a kiss into the air)* Did Dawn start it? *(Mock-throws another kiss)*

TERESA: I'll be perfect. I won't talk to anyone. You can put me in Adjustment, but please don't give me that shot.

DOCTOR: Oh—*(Pulls out an oversize hypodermic needle)* you remember.

TERESA: *(Trying to pull away)* I'm sorry. I'm really sorry. If I had it to do over again, I'd just hold on to that little shit Juanita until the matron came. I would. I promise I would. I didn't mean to hurt her—she's just jealous. She fell. She did this to get me here.

DOCTOR: You did this, Teresa. *(Flips* TERESA *around so the side of her bottom is exposed, rubs it with alcohol)* This should remind you not to fight. *(*DOCTOR *backs up, takes aim with hypo and with a big sweeping movement, lands on target)*

TERESA: *(Cries and pleads)* Please don't give it to me. It makes me feel like I'm dying. Please don't...please...

*(*TERESA *begins to shake all over and gasp for breath—this continues throughout* DOCTOR*'s speech. The injection is a muscle relaxant—the lung muscles are among those affected, so that involuntary [natural] breathing is made impossible, giving patient the feeling of drowning or suffocating.)*

DOCTOR: *(Removing the needle)* You have to learn to act like a lady, Teresa. You can't throw your fists into the face of anyone who does something you don't like. We can't have a world like that, Teresa. Every time you fight, you're going to get one of these.

DOCTOR: *(Holds up hypo, though* TERESA *by this time is gasping for air)* You must calm yourself, and decide you are going to be a lady *(Moves behind net)* and be good and kind to your fellow inmates and to all the people here who have your best interests at heart. You know, Teresa, we have only your best interests at heart. You have to become a lady so that we can help you.

*(*OX TAIL, CHAMP, CYNTHIA *and* EL TORO *wheel a tray of cosmetics toward* TERESA*—they can work with stewardess images. As* DOCTOR *continues her lecture,* PRISONERS *apply eye makeup, rouge, lipstick, spray deodorant, nail polish and perfume to* TERESA*'s body.* TERESA *continues to suffer convulsions and gasp for air—*PRISONERS *help restrain her when the gasping and convulsions get too great. Audience must be allowed to see that the other* PRISONERS *really care for* TERESA*, but that they must follow orders or they might be in her place next.)*

DOCTOR: You have to keep your dress on and stop walking like a cowboy. You have to start wearing the nice lipstick we allow you. You can make enough money working here to buy the nice lipstick and mascara, and hairspray and perfume you're allowed to wear now. *(Note: After orientation* PRISONERS *are given some makeup privileges.)* You know, in the old days, ladies here weren't even permitted to get dressed up and pretty. But now you can go to the beauty parlor and learn to fix your hair real nice in all the latest man-catching styles. You can get yourself real fixed up here, Teresa. So when you get out, if you shape up, you can get yourself a husband and settle down and live like a normal human being. And raise a family and cook and care for your man and all your little children and be kind to the people who want to help you. You want to do that, don't you, Teresa?

TERESA: *(Through gasps and cries, shaking and flailing, the other* PRISONERS *hold her down)* Holy Mary, Mother of...I'm dying. O Mother Mary, Blessed art thou. O Mother Mary, save me, save me *(Gasp for air)* Hail Mary full of grace. *(Gasp)* Mother, I can't breathe—I'm sick and drowning—take me in your arms. I adore you, Holy Mother.

DOCTOR: *(Calmly in control)* If you promise you'll never fight again and will obey all the rules, and understand we are only here to help you and see you develop in your best interests, *(Spreads arms, opens them to heaven in "Christ's ascension" image)* I-will-save-your-life.

TERESA: Mary will save my life!

DOCTOR: *(Maintaining image)* Mary and I will save your life!

TERESA: Only the Mother of God can do that. *(Gasping and convulsions—goes into fit)*

DOCTOR: *(Leaps out from behind net, slowly approaches* TERESA*)* You act like the worst kind of criminal male, Teresa! There is a long list of complaints against you! *(Builds and builds till she loses control)* You cut another woman's face with a home-made knife! You stole baby pictures from Johanna! You beat Juanita till she had to go to the hospital! *(Calming herself, regaining control)* If you don't pull yourself together and start to act like a feminine person, you'll get more of these injections.

TERESA: *(Goes into convulsions—other* PRISONERS *restrain her.)* I can't stand it. I'm dying. Hail Mary full of grace.

DOCTOR: Do you promise never to fight again, Teresa?

*(*TERESA *retches and gasps, the others hold her.)*

DOCTOR: Do you promise to act like a lady?

(Slowly TERESA *and other* PRISONERS *nod in unison.)*

DOCTOR: I can't hear you, Teresa. Answer me like a lady.

(They continue nodding. Others get up and walk like zombies nodding toward their cells. TERESA *remains in chair, nodding.)*

DOCTOR: Do you promise you will become a feminine person, demure and self-controlled? To smile whenever you see me walk by? To control your temper and learn to walk like a sexy woman? Do you promise, Teresa?

*(*TERESA *nods.)*

DOCTOR: I can't hear you. Ladies know how to speak.

TERESA: *(Nodding)* I...pro—mise....

*(*DOCTOR *smiles and injects sedative. Lights dim and come up on* RONNIE*'s cell.* TERESA *crawls to cells on her stomach.)*

RONNIE: *(Shouts to the whole prison yard, especially at* OX TAIL, EL TORO, CYNTHIA *and* CHAMP *who are nodding and walking like zombies)* Awwww, you commie prudes give me a pain where a pill can't reach. Why, if we lived in any of them commie countries, we'd be shot or put in jail.

*(*CHAMP *and others re-enter the present and cross to their cells, no longer zombie-like.)*

CHAMP: Hell, we are in jail.

RONNIE: I mean, we'd be in jail for being gay. Just for that, stupid—'stead of what we are in for. I mean, if I was clean of everything, everything—but just I was gay—they'd shoot me or put me in an insane asylum if I wouldn't go straight.

CHAMP: You'd get proper help.

RONNIE: Goddamn it, that's just what I mean! You think I'm sick! Listen, you nearsighted Marxist. I chose to be gay. I chose a woman to defy the man. It was a political act... *(Raises fist)* ...and... *(Rubs herself on bars)* ...it was a sex act. *(Busts herself up laughing)* Trouble with you guys is, you got zippers on yer pussies, there's padlocks on the zippers, and you have forgot the combination!

CHAMP: You didn't make a political choice—you're just a pitiful victim of a repetition compulsion—

RONNIE: Thank you, Doctor. It's all in my head, so get out of bed! *(A little jivey dance)* It's all in my head so get out of bed! It's all in my head so get out of—

*(*OX TAIL *enters, transformed into* MATRON, *faces cells from center of yard area.)*

MATRON: Bedtime.

*(Plays "bell sound" violin chord—*PRISONERS *come forward in their cells for the count.)*

JOCKEY: Six.

CHAMP: Twelve.

KATHLEEN: Sixteen.

CYNTHIA: Twenty-nine.

EL TORO: Thirty-one.

RONNIE: Forty.

MATRON: Lock in! *(Rattles chain on cells to signify lock-up)* Lights out!

(Blackout)

*(*CYNTHIA *puts on guard coat and transforms into the* WARDEN. *She suspends herself over to one set of scaffold cells to give the god-like quality of looking down on the prisoners. Her voice becomes a tinny drone— by desensualizing the voice she sounds like a loudspeaker. She does not hear the women—nor is she aware of the activity [the passing of contraband] going on inside the cells. The* PRISONERS *hear the* WARDEN'*s voice and go about their covert activities, cautiously passing cigarettes, dirty magazines, a vibrator, valium, etc.)*

(The next scene, "Harriet the Snitch" begins as soon as the WARDEN *speaks. Both scenes play simultaneously and can be heard clearly. Visually, the main focus is on the active passing of contraband.)*

WARDEN: Welcome to the Women's State Correctional Facility. There are rules to be followed here. I will give you the daily routine, rules and general procedures of our institution.
5:00 A M. Awake culinary workers
5:30 A M. You will be counted
6:00 A M. Awake entire population to prepare for breakfast
7:00 A M. Breakfast
7:30 A M. All inmates report to place of work assignment
8:00 A M. You will be counted
11:30 A M. Dinner
12 noon. You will be counted
12:30 P M. All inmates return to place of work assignment
3:00 P M. Prepare to return to living spaces
3:30 P M. You will be counted
4:30 P M. Supper
5:30 P M. You will be counted
6:30 P M. Recreation: T V, cards and outside recreation, weather permitting
7:30 P M. You will be counted
10:00 P M. Lights out
10:30 P M. You will be counted

(Simultaneously with the above speech, twinkle lights come up on cells where the women are cautiously passing contraband.)

CHAMP: *(Handing a small packet to* CYNTHIA*)* Here's your Thorazine and Librium. That's a pack.

CYNTHIA: *(Passes a pack of cigarettes to* CHAMP *in payment)* One pack. Thanks.

KATHLEEN: Stash it all—here comes the snitch!!

*(*JOCKEY *transformed into* HARRIET, *the prison snitch, enters her cell, smiling and waving to the others.)*

CHAMP: *(To the others)* Watch her. She'll make you think she wants you for her old man, and then go rat on you to the screw.

(The women become very busy and ignore HARRIET.*)*

HARRIET: *(Trying to wiggle her way into the conversation)* Oh Juanita, you have the most beautiful hair. Teresa, hasn't Juanita the most beautiful hair you ever saw?

OX TAIL: Some have and some haven't.

HARRIET: Who's got a coffin nail? *(Silence)* I'm dying for a smoke. That movie they had tonight is the squarest they've had since I been in.

CHAMP: You mean you can tell the difference?

HARRIET: Hey, Dana, baby—I just love to say your real name, Dana—hey Dana baby, don't get on me, I love you. I been digging you ever since you arrived—I think you're neat. I really get off on your attitude—I'd give anything to be like you.

CHAMP: Some can and some can't.

HARRIET: I mean it, Dana. I even try to copy your walk.

CHAMP: They throw people in the hole for less than that.

HARRIET: Aww, they're not that bad, Dana. You always try to make out the staff so mean.

CHAMP: I don't do nothin—they show the world.

HARRIET: *(Laughing)* You break me up.

CHAMP: I didn't notice anything funny. *(To others)* Did you notice anything funny I said?

KATHLEEN: I didn't notice that you said anything funny.

HARRIET: Hey, can I have a piece of the action?

OTHER PRISONERS: *(Freezing her out)* Some can and some can't.

*(*PRISONERS *fall into images of caged animals. The twinkle lights blink on and off as the women transform from one caged image to another. These may be a combination of still and moving images. Some images may have appeared earlier in the play. The* WARDEN *never breaks the pattern of her speech. [At O M T it was always about here that the "snitch" scene was completed and the images began.])*

WARDEN: 11:45 P M. You will be counted
2:00 A M. You will be counted

You must keep your blouses buttoned to the top button, keep your collar out. You must eat all food you take at feeding time—all food. You will not make any comment on what goes on in our institution or about another inmate in letters sent out of our institution. You will never use vulgar and/or profane language. Only two people at a time may sit on a bed, and they must be sitting up with both feet on the floor. You may not speak to a visitor without permission. You will not whistle, laugh loudly or talk loud. You will always be neat and clean. You will refrain from combing your hair in the recreation room.

EL TORO: *(Comes to the front of her cell and shouts to the others)* They won't let us have nothing juicy to read!

KATHLEEN: *(Pounding on cell bars, responding to* EL TORO*)* Oh, what I'd give for a hot and nasty R Crumb Comix.

CHAMP: *(At the front of her cell)* Hey, if I had a hot and dirty book to read, you think they would read it with me over the watchdog T V? Or would they come and snatch it away and read it all alone by their lonesomes in the matrons' john?

OX TAIL: *(To the others)* We could share the wealth, but they wouldn't do that, I bet— oh no!

*(*JOCKEY*, as herself again, leaps out of her cell to the center playing area and strips down to her shorts and "coyote" T-shirt. [Whether the actor strips is a directorial choice.])*

JOCKEY: But hey, what if I croon a dirty book to you? They couldn't take it away, hey? No, there'd be nothing for 'em to confiscate. Nothing to go against me in my file for the parole board, because it would go right out into the air.

(Acts out the "dirty book" story as she "croons" it, transforming into a pop-art version of the aggressive male. Simultaneously the others change clothes and transform into their favorite criminals from the past.)

JOCKEY: Oh, he sighed as he stared at the juicy melons straining in their titty-tight circular-stitched Egyptian cotton bra. Oh, he cried inside his head. Oh, I want to get my hot and pulsating hands inside her shocking pink low-cut cleavage, and free those two giant cantaloupes from their cloth cages. Yes, he husked into her perfectly carved alabaster ear. Yes, my dewy angel. Yes, I love you with all my heart and soul. He felt his member swelling, compelling him toward his goal. He crushed her shocking-pink -sheathed, hot and heaving body, and ran his long, hair-matted hands down to the bottom of her bottom. And his tongue reared up in his mouth as he gazed upon the outline of her twin love buttons, pushing forward, begging to escape into his loving lips. But first he nibbled softly at the base of her neck. Softly, softly, softly. We got all night together, angel of my life. I'm going to graze my mouth over the length and breast of you before I unsheath my own pink knife.

(Lights come up on RONNIE *in her cell dressed as her dream crook. The* OTHERS *stand behind her in costumes of their fantasies—the Watergate men, Al Capone, Bonnie, etc. During* RONNIE'S *next speech, the* OTHERS *transform into specific contemporary criminals and ask, plead or demand to be pardoned.)*

RONNIE: When my mother and sisters	
find out what you've done to me,	OX TAIL: Pardon me!
they're gonna run all the way	
from home,	KATHLEEN: Pardon me!
and tear this concentration camp	JOCKEY & EL TORO: Pardon me!
out by the roots	
and throw it, bars and all, into	
the Gulf of Mexico. They won't	
let you do this to me.	CYNTHIA: Pardon me!
My mother loves me.	OX TAIL: Pardon me.
My sisters love me.	EL TORO: Pardon me.
My mother always loved me.	KATHLEEN & JOCKEY: Pardon me.
And when she finds out you took	
her daughter away from her,	CYNTHIA: Pardon me!
she's gonna set fire to your	
feet, she's gonna set fire to	
your liver, she's gonna set	
fire to your eyes, and she's	
gonna laugh while you scream	
for her mercy.	OX TAIL & JOCKEY: Pardon me.
You can't do this to her daughter	
(Name calling) You Jesus-	
Freak cocksuckers! You Nazis.	
You rusty I-U-D's. You beer cans.	
You leaky diaphragms. You WASP	
lickers, you ass-kissers of the	
State! *(Pause)* Let me out	
of here before my mother finds	KATHLEEN: Pardon me.
out what you're doing to me.	EL TORO: Pardon me.
This is your last chance.	CYNTHIA: Pardon me.
You're gonna get it, you're	
really gonna get it.	OX TAIL: Pardon me.
My mother and my sisters	
love me!	

(PRISONERS begin speak-singing "pardon me" from their cells, each on own dissonant note.)

JOCKEY: Pardon me!

EL TORO: Pardon me!

ALL: Pardon me!

RONNIE: Oh gee, pardon me.

CHAMP: Oh see Spot. Pardon me.

OX TAIL & CYNTHIA: Oh we saw him—Gerry Ford—Pardon the bastards.

JOCKEY: I got caught!

ALL: I got caught,
But I wasn't meant to—

EL TORO: They caught the ones in the right spot.

CHAMP & RONNIE: But *they* didn't mean it.

ALL: We all know *they* didn't mean it.

OX TAIL, CYNTHIA & KATHLEEN:
They only had *their* best interests at heart,
And they don't want to be apart
From their wives and daughters.

JOCKEY, RONNIE & CHAMP: They sure as fucking far-out won't change their spots!

JOCKEY: Pardon me.

EL TORO: Pardon me.

OX TAIL: Pardon me.

CYNTHIA: Pardon me.

RONNIE: You caught me red-handed but I didn't do it!

KATHLEEN: So, you better—

CYNTHIA: Pardon me.

CHAMP: Pardon me.

RONNIE: Pardon me.

ALL: Pardon me! *(Beat)* Pardon me! *(Beat)* Par-don-ME!!!!

(All hold)

(Blackout)

END OF PLAY

VIET ROCK

is dedicated to the IDEA of the United States of America.

VIET ROCK (a folk-war movie) was first produced by the Open Theatre and Ellen Stewart at Cafe LaMama on Second Avenue, N Y C on 21 May 1966, Armed Forces Day. The cast and creative contributors were:

Seth Allen
Shami Chaikin
Fred Forrest
Sharon Gans
Robert Hart
John Kramer
Marcia Jean Kurtz
Nina Levin
Roy London
Muriel Miguel
Suzanne Pred
Barbara Ralley
Gerome Ragni
Howard Roy
Alice Tweedie
Jack Tatarskey

Directors .... Peter Feldman, Joseph Chaikin, and Megan Terry
Composer, Conductor, Piano .... Marianne de Pury
Designer .... Esther Gilman
Soundtape .... Marianne de Pury
Lights .... Lee Levine, Maggie Dominic

The directors thank Gwen Fabricant, John Wendell and Don Walters for their assistance in the preparation of this production.

The play then opened the Yale School of Drama season, produced by the School of Drama under the direction of Robert Brustein, and The Open Theatre on 11 October 1966, in New Haven, CT. The cast and creative contributors were:

Seth Allen
Kay Carney
Jordan Charney
Shami Chaikin
Joseph Daly
Fred Forrest
Sharon Gans
Paul Giovanni
Marcia Jean Kurtz
Roy London
Muriel Miguel
Gerome Ragni
Barbara Ralley

Director .... Megan Terry
Score & musician .... Marianne de Pury
Set & lighting .... Gil Wechsler
Costume crew .... Santo Loquasto, Phylis Preston & Carolyn Ross
Sound .... Paul Jaeger

The song *Viet Rock* was sung by Fred Forrest with guitar accompaniment by The Mushrooms.

On 10 November 1966, the play, directed by Megan Terry, opened at the Martinique Theater in New York City, produced by Jordan Charney, Nancy Cooperstein and David Rothenberg.

On 26 November 1966, A B C network televised twenty minutes of the play nationally under the title *Viet Rock: Play Of Protest*, produced by James Benjamin and Thomas H Wolf, for A B C News. The commentator was Howard K Smith, who also interviewed the author.

PRODUCTION NOTES

VIET ROCK was developed in my Saturday Workshop at the Open Theater. It grew out of improvisation, combined with the exploration of acting techniques discovered and perfected by Joseph Chaikin in his Monday Workshops.

We used material that bombarded us every day from television and newspapers. We acted out personal stories and tried to get at the roots of our drives toward anger and aggression. To deal with the bewilderment, shame, and confusion created by this war, I felt we had to explore our negative feelings, drives, and fantasies. I worked to expose these qualities, then formalized them. Also, we explored loss, grief, and regret. We tried to get at the essence of violence.

Out of the material surfacing from this work I made the play, and we began to rehearse it. Most of the staging came naturally out of the content. The director must keep in mind that the visual images here are more important than the words.

Marianne de Pury, the composer, worked with me from the very first exercises. The music grew along with the play and is still developing.

As work progressed, we found we could get strong values by playing the scenes with an attitude of light irony. This builds a certain driving ruthlessness, which must not become heavy. If the right balance is maintained, the audience will become involved intellectually, emotionally, and kinesthetically. Audience involvement is necessary and must be there to make the play work.

Every positive and comic value in the play must be played, and then the dark values will come through with twice the impact.

I had written and designed VIET ROCK to be played at Ellen Stewart's Cafe La Mama Experimental Theater Club. This is a small, long narrow room, with low ceilings. To make maximum use of this space the audience was seated in bleacher-like formations on either side of the playing area, and some of the action takes place directly on the floor. The actors almost constantly address the audience, and this had vivid impact in such close quarters.

When we were asked to take the play to other stages and spaces like Yale, I feared the impact would be less. I was wrong. The play takes on more dimension with increase of space and audience size. The audience can't enjoy the individual actors to the same close extent, but the accumulative aspects of the play seem even more crushing on a bigger stage.

It is most necessary that the director make maximum use of the playing area and concentrate not only on the intent of the scene but the emotional content—is it being felt by the audience in how it looks to them? Lighting can be most helpful here, especially in proscenium with black curtains. It's gratifying to know that the play works no matter what the space. But one should never lose sight of the fact that it grew out of, and is ultimately playing against, world events. Some of my fellow writers berated me for not writing something more timeless. Luckily this comment did not shock me into silence.

The only scenery—two benches and four chairs. The men should be dressed in blue work clothes and boots, and the women in free-flowing dresses or skirts and tights. As many actors should be employed as the director feels confident to work with. I had from thirteen to sixteen and would have liked more.

THE SETTING

Posted around the theater, if the director wishes, or worked into the setting, should be the following phrases. It would be good if the audience could see them before the play begins. They should not be spotlighted or illuminated in any way. But just woven in here and there. After all, they are with us every day of this war.

Offense Action Yell Freedumb Enter Killer Trainees Men of Good Will The New Army Viet Nam Hangs Over Your Head The Ultimate Weapon Victor-Charlies Action Freebies Get It Over With Bulldozer Pow-we Specie? Eat Dickhead You Yankee? V-C The End Is Ongoing Freedom Hi Sweetheart! Sell Out Vigorous and Optimistic Gut Hanging Out Her Son Racist Your Name's on It Flirt with Her Hit Up Out The Up and Down Way Pleads I Say Your Name Back Play Her Game Hawk-Dove-Owl-Worms Our Little Yellow Brothers Is There a Sign? Round Eyes A Position in the World Contain Die Away Treesies Win the Balls Game A Whole Man Make Love Oriental Needs Us as Enemy Concentration Escalation Mouth Your Tongue Believe History Deploy Tactics Into Bed Out East Pretentions Non-White Withdrew Withdraw Withdrawn Advance Dissent Respectable Hot The Never Again Club Playmate of the Month Limited War Our Society Your Rights Rough Days Ahead for Him Alternative Patriot Your Turn The Path We're On I Have Been Wrong Political Future Mortal Fear Not His Job Half a Century Fire His Truth Is Marching On Sense of Duty Revolutionary War War of 1812 Civil War Indian Wars Spanish-American War Cave War WWI&II&K Love War Stomp Short Order War Words Are Actions A Kill-In Bombed-Out Messages Peace Efforts At Home Wholesale Price Index Up A Threat-In Bless Your Heart Feeding Her People Happening-Frustration Hold Debate Length Possible Nastiness Difficulty Hawkish Distress Trouble Standstill Thrashing Face Belligerent Against Unwilling Upset Withdraw Where In the Throes Bankrupt Tendencies Process 90MM Recoiliess Rifle No Time to Myself Infant-ry God Love Ya One Man Cannon Balls The Kid Our Commitments Own Special Interests Bland Terms Do What We Have To Do Where Does Your Image Hurt Now? Practice Dummies The Hand of God "Eee-ya," He Screamed Lost His Grip Wanta Bite? Peacekeeper of the World Under Bird No Kidding Put Your Lives on the Line Hip-in Hi Joe! You and Yours I Dreamed I Saw J F K Last Night, Alive as You and Me Never Mind the Rain—Eat Mud You're a Riot Alice Too Young What the Hell Is That? Prop-a-Gandhi Reject

Ancient Quarrels Ring Dang Doo AcceptHonor Zappppppppppppp Pledge Do—For Your Country YER A BUNCH OF NERVOUS NELLIES

ACT ONE

(As audience is getting settled actors begin to appear, one by one or in pairs. They lie down on the stage. When everyone is settled there is a short silence. As lights begin to dim, song is heard on tape. It should be played once before action begins.)

VOICE: *(Singing* The Viet Rock*)*
Far across the Southern Sea
Is a land where Viets rock.
Here every morning you can see
The Viets roll.
When the bombs fall,
The Viets rock and rock.
When the napalm bursts,
Then the Viets roll.
At the sound of jets,
The Viets rock and rock.
When the tracers flash,
Then the Viets roll.
Rock and roll, rock and roll,
How the sweet Viets
Love to rock and roll.
Those dear little Viets
Love our rock and roll.
Do the Viet Rock,
Watch that Viet roll.
Do the Viet Rock,
Watch that Viet roll.
That's the way the Viets rock,
All the way the Viets roll.
Rock and roll, rock and roll,
Do the Viet Rock.

(As lights dim up, the actors are discovered lying on the floor in a circle. Their bodies, heads inward, form a giant flower or a small target. They are still; bit by bit movement can be detected. First: as if flower petals are stirred by wind or are warming toward the sun.)

A VOICE ON TAPE: *(Recites the following)* Things could be different. Nobody wins. We are teams of losers. Whatever doesn't kill you makes you stronger. Or isn't life the dream of those who are dying? It's only by virtue of our eyes that there are stars. I've been a long time a-comin' and I'll be a long time gone. Let us persevere in what we have resolved before we forget. Look out for number one. What you don't know can kill you.

(Silence. Viet Rock *is heard on tape again. Silence. From circle of bodies we hear humming or gurgling. Sound rises bit by bit, at times leaps into laughter and childlike sound of delight. The sounds should be joyous, aggressive, like those children make when playing vigorous games, but in no way should the actors try to give their impressions of sounds they think children make. This is cloying and irritating. The sound must come from their past, but the voices must come from inside and not be forced. The actors should have worked to free their imaginations before the play begins. What happens in the first ten minutes on the floor should take on the character of group free association, to represent a tribal recall of ancient scenes and events. Playtime material, especially of war games, cowboys and Indians, cops and robbers, should be allowed to come to the surface and explode into sound, sounds of weapons, horses, tanks, planes, guns, troops, orders, marching, bugles, songs, etc. The tenor of the sound should be one of joyful mastery, and imaginative striving to succeed in a frightening situation. Once the sound begins to build, the actors keep each other going: they must listen to each other. The sound should rise to a climax and end in one final burst of chord sound. As the explosive sound begins to fall, they should turn on their bellies, crawl toward center, and reach out for each other. They talk to each other in a bubbly way and, holding hands, slowly rise together. This makes a beautiful shape, round but changing. They keep their heads down to maintain shape. As they rise, they begin to move in a circle. The circle begins to bounce. The sound is teasing and full of fun; when they are nearly erect the circle should bounce up and down in unison. When it reaches a climax, the circle should explode, flinging the actors around the floor, laughing. They stay in place, laughing at each other. There is an instant transformation. The male actors become new babies, and the female actors become mothers. The women find the nearest baby boy on the floor and kneel down to play with their baby. The only words they may use are "mama" and "baby." The women begin to undress the men lovingly, playing with the babies and kissing them. They continue this until all the men are stripped to their shorts. The feeling should be one of play, discovery, and contentment. As soon as he is stripped, the actor who will play the* SERGEANT *in the play leaps to his feet and yells:)*

SERGEANT: Ten-Hut!

(The men leap to their feet and assemble into lines for an army physical. Several women become cold, impersonal doctors and perform an examining ritual on the men. Two women sit in chairs facing the audience. As each man is O Kd they look at a person in the audience and announce:)

WOMEN: U S Government Inspected Male.

(The men in the line jump to two doctors. When the audience is on two sides of the action, two sets of doctors should be used. The men are commanded to jump, cough, and bend over while they receive shots. When they bend over the two doctors give them a swat. At the sound of the swat the women facing the audience make their announcement.)

DOCTORS: *(Sing)* Jump cough bend.

MEN: *(Sing)* Stick him in the arm,
Stick him in the end. *(Repeat)*

WOMEN: *(Sing)* U S Government Inspected Male!

DOCTORS: *(Sing)* Jump cough bend.

MEN: *(Sing)* Stick him in the arm,
Stick him in the end. *(Repeat)*

WOMEN: *(Sing)* U S Government Inspected Male!

DOCTORS: *(Sing)* Jump cough bend.

MEN: *(Sing)* Stick him in the ass
And see if he'll mend. *(Repeat)*

DOCTORS: *(Sing)* Jump cough bend.

WOMEN: *(Sing)* U S Government Inspected Male!

MEN: *(Sing)* JIGGLE HIS BALLS
And see if he'll blend.

DOCTORS: *(Sing)* Jump cough bend.

MEN: *(Sing)* Jump cough bend,
Stick it in the arm
But you'll get it in the end. *(Repeat)*

WOMEN: U S Government Inspected Male!

(Two mothers in a coffee shop near Whitehall Street wait for their sons who are being examined for induction. They play their scene very big, very fast, seated to the side of the stage, brightly lit. A low drumbeat begins.)

MRS SHERMAN :*(Nervous and fidgety; to break her tension she tries to start a conversation)* Ah, do you have the time?

MRS COLE: *(Cold)* Yes.

MRS SHERMAN: That's nice.

MRS COLE: There's a clock on the wall.

MRS SHERMAN: Oh, so there is. I didn't notice.

*(*MRS COLE *shrugs and turns away.* MRS SHERMAN*'s tension mounts.)*

MRS SHERMAN: It's a long wait.

*(*MRS COLE *gives her a "what the hell do you mean?" look.* MRS SHERMAN *nods.)*

MRS SHERMAN: It's such a long wait in a short time like this.

*(*MRS COLE *turns away.)*

MRS SHERMAN: I can't stand to think of him in there with all the rest of them, being treated like a piece of meat.

(MRS COLE turns more severely away.)

MRS SHERMAN: How old is your boy?

MRS COLE: I beg your pardon?

MRS SHERMAN: Your son?

MRS COLE: What?

MRS SHERMAN: I, oh, excuse me, I thought you were waiting for your son like I am.

MRS COLE: I'm drinking coffee.

MRS SHERMAN: I'm sorry, but I'm nervous. Aren't you nervous?

MRS COLE: Why should I be nervous?

MRS SHERMAN: Well, if your boy was being examined by the army this very minute, wouldn't you be nervous?

MRS COLE: He is.

MRS SHERMAN: But you said you were only drinking coffee.

MRS COLE: I am.

(MRS SHERMAN gives her a bewildered look.)

MRS COLE: They won't take him.

MRS SHERMAN: Something wrong with him?

MRS COLE: There's nothing wrong with him. He's perfect.

MRS SHERMAN: Oh yeah?

MRS COLE: *(Looking at watch)* He should be here any minute. It won't take them long to make up their minds.

MRS SHERMAN: You got pull, eh?

MRS COLE: They wouldn't take my Laird. He'd be terrible in a jungle.

MRS SHERMAN: I know they'll take Ralphie. I just know it. He's built fifty forts on our fire escape. He knows everything about building forts.

MRS COLE: That'll come in handy.

MRS SHERMAN: He'll be protecting the freedom of your son.

MRS COLE: Some have to go.

MRS SHERMAN: He'll be fighting for your little boy.

MRS COLE: I can't help that. God didn't designate my Laird to be a fighter.

MRS SHERMAN: You do it for him, eh?

MRS COLE: The strong have to protect the weak.

MRS SHERMAN: It isn't fair. My Ralphie's A-I, er I-A. He was such a little baby. You wouldn't believe. He only weighed four pounds and two ounces when he was born. Such an easy birth. It was my husband gave all the trouble. We had to run to the hospital. The car wouldn't start. Ralphie was born in the emergency receiving room. He wouldn't wait.

*(*MRS COLE *looks up to see her son coming toward her. While this happens the other men continue dressing at one side of the stage.)*

LAIRD: Hi hi hi, M-M-M-M-Mom.

MRS COLE: Laird. What the hell are you wearing?

LAIRD: I'm I'm I'm I'm...

MRS COLE: No.

LAIRD: Yes.

MRS COLE: They wouldn't.

LAIRD *(Smiling)*: M-M-M-M-M-M-Mom, I made it.

MRS COLE: But how could they?

LAIRD: They like me, M-M-M-M-M-Mom, I'mmmm All Am-Am-Am-American.

*(*MRS SHERMAN *sees* RALPHIE *coming toward her.)*

RALPHIE: Hi, Mom.

MRS COLE: *(Hugging* LAIRD *and crying)* Oh, Baby.

MRS SHERMAN: Ralphie! *(She pulls him to her.)* Tell me?

RALPHIE: It's O K, Mom. Mom, there was this guy in there he was so... Oh... *(Seeing* LAIRD *in his mother's arms)* There he is! They're getting desperate, Mom... But...

MRS SHERMAN: Something's wrong. Tell me. Ralphie. I can feel it.

RALPHIE: *(Kisses her on the cheek)* I'm going to be all right. I just have to go to the hospital a couple days.

MRS SHERMAN: Oh, Ralphie, you have blood in your urine! You have blood in your urine!

RALPHIE: I'm in the army. It's O K. I'll just have to go to the hospital a couple of days.

MRS SHERMAN: *(Hugging and kissing* RALPHIE*)* You get rid of that blood.
(Sings)
Now that you are up so tall
I have to share you with the world,

But I can't be nice all the time,
I get mad and up comes my gall.

Goodbye, my good boy,
Goodbye, my good boy.
Go quick,
Mother promised not to cry.

But if you have to go
I got to give you strength.
I won't chicken out
And I won't shrink.

But I don't like it,
Why can't I fight it?
Goodbye, my good boy,
Goodbye, my dear,
Goodbye, my good boy,
Mother holds you here.

I lost too many already
And now it comes again.
But I don't like it,
Why can't I fight it?

The wars have melted into one,
A war was on when I was born
Will this be on when I am done?
That kind of triple feature, please God save me from.
Goodbye, my good boy,
Goodbye, my love,
Goodbye, my good boy, I wish you weren't old enough.

RALPHIE: Goodbye, Mom.

(RALPHIE *then kisses* MRS COLE *goodbye. All the other male actors line up to kiss* MRS SHERMAN *goodbye. They each make a different character adjustment to her. Then they all kiss* MRS COLE *goodbye. They kiss all the females goodbye. The women doctors have now turned into mothers or sweethearts and sit on benches. While this action takes place one woman sings to the audience while sitting on a chair. As the song ends the* SERGEANT *yells.)*

SERGEANT: Fall in. Ten-hut!

(The men get into an awkward line. The SERGEANT *snaps them up. The following should be an accelerated drill course.)*

SERGEANT: I hate recruits! Now listen, you mens, and listen good. The army is going to train you mens to become ultimate weapons. Is that clear?

(The men nod.)

SERGEANT: Is that clear?

(They nod again. This makes the SERGEANT *very angry.)*

SERGEANT: Answer me like you got a pair!

G IS: *(Scream)* Yes, Sergeant!

*(*SERGEANT *is satisfied.)*

SERGEANT: *(Continuing his drill course)* Left face. Right face. About face. Right face!

(The men make mistakes and the SERGEANT *corrects them with tense enjoyment)*

SERGEANT: Left face, right face. About face. Right face. About face. *(One of the men does not please him. He calls him out of line.)* You, Allen, get out here. The rest of you men watch.

(The men rush to watch. The SERGEANT *is angry.)*

SERGEANT: Fall in! In place—watch! Don't move! Don't move, girls. Allen. In place march!

(He marches in stylized fashion. The SERGEANT *is almost nose to nose with him.)*

SERGEANT: Allen, in place double time.

*(*ALLEN *marches faster and faster.)*

SERGEANT: Company halt, one two.

(The soldier makes one more foot fall than he should and the SERGEANT *glares him back to his place.)*

SERGEANT: Fall in. In place march. Left face, in place march. About face. Right face.

(He gets them back facing him.)

SERGEANT: All right, girlies, you're in the army now. Sound off!

G IS: One two.

SERGEANT: Sound off!

G IS: Three, four.

SERGEANT: Cadence count.

G IS: One two three four, one-two, three four!

SERGEANT: O K. Girlies, forward march!

(They march around the stage as he eyes them carefully.)

SERGEANT: Company halt! Very good, girlies. One day you'll become ladies. Ten-hut. O K, girlies, we're going to do some push-ups. At ease. Fall into place.

(The men fall down in push-up positions.)

SERGEANT: One. Two. Three. Four. Five.

*(*SERGEANT *fades back to watch their form. During the push-up formation, the man speaking the line is up, and the others are flat against the floor. They should go up and down when their line comes up.)*

G I ONE: You know that all young men have to face a time in life when they have to make their own decisions. when they have to put Momma's voice aside and when they have to face up.

G I TWO: Well, that time came to me, that time that all young men must face up to.

G I THREE: This is the time that I call the breaking point.

GI FOUR: This is the time when the young man puts away childish things, like childhood and Momma's voice so that he can step out into the world a man.

G I FIVE: I chose to make my own foot felt by walking through the door of the induction center.

G I SIX: That's what I call marking my breaking point.

G I SEVEN: I didn't have to get anybody's O K, no names signed beside my one.

G I EIGHT: It was my thing to do.

G I ONE: So I put my foot down on the threshold to manhood and put away my childhood.

G I TWO: And now as I go through life, I...

(All men are up in top of push-up position for this speech.)

ALL G IS: ...Pray to my sergeant that I may be a man to man.
I pray to my sergeant that I may be a man to sergeant
I pray to my sergeant that I may be a man to country.
I pray to my sergeant that I may be a man to Mother.
I pray to my sergeant that I may be a man to Dog.
I pray to my sergeant that I may be a man to God.

SERGEANT: All right, girls. Ten-hut! *(He sings to them:* War Au Go Go.)
Come my ladies, take your rifles
Here my bunnies are grenadies,
Stand to battle,
Little pussies.
War au go go
Is our game.

That's my sweethearts, War au go go,
Get your back up,
War au go go,
War au go go
Is our game.

Come, my girlies,
Suck in your tummies
To win your stripies,
Act like ladies,
Because it's war au go go
For my girlies.
War au go go
For my babes.
War au go go, War au go go,
War au go go
Is our game.

Grip your rifles, little bunnies,
Throw grenadies, little ladies.
Run to battle,
Little pussies.
War au go go
Is our game.
War au go go, little honeys.
War au go go,
Smarten up, you dames!
War au go go,
War au go go,
War au go go,
Is our game.

War au go go!

(Everyone comes in on "War au go go's")

SERGEANT: All right, ladies. Fall in! Ten-hut! *(He sings)*
You're in the army now,
You're not atop a cow....

G IS & WOMEN: *(Sitting on benches)*
You'll never get rich,
You son-of-a-bitch,
You're in the shit-house now!

SERGEANT: Sound off!

G IS: One two.

SERGEANT: Sound off.

G IS: Three four.

SERGEANT: Cadence count.

G IS: One two three four, one-two, three-four!

(The SERGEANT inspects them and might slap or snap at one whose button is wrong, etc.)

G Is: Ten-hut! Forward march!

(They march across the stage, filling it. They reach the other side.)

SERGEANT: *(Yells)* Halt. Left face.

(As they do, all the female actors with arms linked rush on and fall down in a kneeling position ranged across center stage.)

SERGEANT: *(Yells)* About face, forward march.

(As the men make an about-face and march forward, they stumble over the women. Muffled sounds of "Broads! Hey, Sarge, look at these lovelies" etc)

G I ONE: Hi, darlin! *(He grabs a girl.)* You come to see me off? *(He stoops to kiss her.)*

SERGEANT: *(Pulling him off by seat of his pants and throwing him back into the line)* That's a protester, you dogbody, you piss-headed lassie!

G I ONE: She ain't mine? Sergeant!

SERGEANT: *(Slapping him)* Straighten up and shut up, girlie!

HEAD PROTESTER: *(At end of line, she lifts her head and calls out to the* SERGEANT*)* Sir, I hereby inform you that you are hereby under citizen's arrest by a citizen of these United States. You are charged, sir, with genocide, criminal conspiracy, and carrying on a full-scale war under the guise of an "expeditionary force."

SERGEANT:Take that pink mitt off this Government property.

PROTESTER: If you will come quietly, sir, I can guarantee you the same fair trial that was conducted in Nuremberg and Israel.

SERGEANT: You are bruising two-hundred-and-fifty-thousand dollars worth of Government training and experience. I suggest you lie down there with your friends where we can crush you all at once.

PROTESTER: "Let you hear me gentle cousin, Westmoreland." Listen, Dog Tag number 1-0-7-7-8-6-6, I have arrested you in the name of morality, Christianity, and sanity!

*(*SERGEANT *looks at protesters and starts laughing. He goes down his line of men and digs each one in ribs till each man laughs at women during their chanting.)*

HEAD PROTESTER: Citizen's arrest...!

ALL PROTESTERS: Stop the war in Vietnam. Make love, not war. BRING OUR BOYS HOME. Stop the war in Vietnam. Make love, not war. Bring our boys home. Stop the war in Vietnam. Make love, not war. Bring our boys home.

SERGEANT: *(Shouting at protesters)* You aren't worth me stomping my boot on. The army is the instrument of the will of the people. That's "consensus" to you, mushheads. Go back to U S History 101. Have you forgotten the Indian Wars already? What country are you really from?

(While the SERGEANT *has been saying the above speech, three of the women protesters have left the line of women and have taken up a position elsewhere on stage. During the following they mime pouring gasoline on themselves and light a real wooden match.)*

PROTESTERS: *(Kneeling with arms linked, they face the soldiers)* We ask you to stop this merciless war.

G IS: *(Shouting as if answering a superior officer)* We didn't start it!

PROTESTERS: Innocent people on all sides are being maimed and murdered.

G IS: *(Shouting)* Sorry about that!

PROTESTERS: Homes are destroyed and people uprooted.

G IS: Downright sorry about that!

PROTESTERS: Join us and stay home.

G IS: We'd like to stay home, but we must serve.

PROTESTERS: Innocent people are being burned.

G IS: Gee, we really are sorry about that!

PROTESTERS: Is that your final answer?

G IS: We have a job to do. There can be no questions.

(The three women strike the wooden matches, whip the lighted matches up and down. The matches go out, and the women are burned. They fall to the floor, jerking and moaning, in final stages of death. The G IS *stand flinty at attention. The* SERGEANT *is furious.)*

SERGEANT: *(To men)* What you standing with yer faces hanging out, ladies? Police the area! On the double!

(Men brutally drag all the women to the benches and throw them down. Women quietly take sitting position on benches while the men start to grind the ashes from the bodies of the three into the ground the way they'd try to get rid of cigarette ashes inadvertently dropped on their mothers' rugs.)

SERGEANT: Fall in! Ten-hut!

*(*G IS *form up into the ultra-erect straight line. At the* SERGEANT*'s nod, one by one they jump out of line and address the audience.)*

G I ONE: What a pity it is that we have what you can apply to some guys the implication "draft dodger." *(He jumps back to place.)*

G I TWO: *(Jumping out)* Some of these dodgers even burn their bodies and cards of the draft.

G I THREE: I believe some of these activities are called "protest moves."

G I FOUR: Now I ask you, how could our forefathers who bled all over this ground that I'm standing on here, how could they not roll around in the hallowed ground of their graves?

G I FIVE: I ask you?

G I SIX: These here are immature actions of these so-called American youth.

G I SEVEN: If our forefathers heard about this, they'd grab up their rusty muskets and rise up from their graves and shoot down the whole bunch of these here so-called American youths who are protesting our so-called Vietnam war.

G I EIGHT: These aren't so-called youths.

G I ONE: These are sneaking subversive commies, that's what they are.

G I FOUR: I suggest to these so-called guys they should take some time off from their burning and do a little deep study of this here problem like I've paid attention to it.

G I TWO: If they won't I suggest we put 'em on a fast boat to Commie China.

G I THREE: I'll pay half the fare myself.

G I FIVE: Just because you don't...

G I SIX: ...Agree with your country...

G I SEVEN: ...Doesn't mean you shouldn't...

G I EIGHT: ...Do what they tell you to.

ALL: *(Jumping out)* And that's all I have to say to these so-called youths.

SERGEANT: *(He turns to address the audience)* These punks, these commies, these bleeding hearts. They're so dumb, they're tools of the pinko reds. These guys who claim to be pacifists—these—they are consumed by war. Do you see them fighting against cancer? No, they're consumed with making exhibits of themselves. Do you see them throwing their bodies down in front of the Detroit assembly lines? That's where some bellyaching is needed. I'd help them protest the frigging motorcars. Ain't a one of them that's not more deadly every day actually than the myth of the BOMB. More bastards bleed their guts out and grind their bones on the cement of our highways than ever lose a piece of snot in Vietnam. These punks is consumed with war. They are against war. Methinks they protest too much. They're scared if they had a legal gun in their hands they'd blow off every head in sight. Maybe their own. They're a bunch of potential suicides and they work it off by protesting us, and making out they're smarter than us, and more humanitarian and such. Let me ask you where we'd all be if we hadn't fought in World War One, World War Two, and Korea? Dead in our beds. That's where. You punks wouldn't even a been a gleam in yer old man's eye, 'cause yer old man woulda been dead before he could get it up. They should get out and fight and get it out of their guts. Since when is it not honorable to die for your country? Spill your blood, boobies. That's the highest form of love. Give your blood for others. These guys is afraid to look at war. You have to fight now to prevent the big one. These crybabies who're afraid of the bomb are asking for it. Thank God there's some men left in America. These bleeding hearts are afraid to look at death. Death isn't so bad. It's very, very peaceful. I mean real death, with real guts strewn about the ground. Real ashes of real houses burned to the dirt. Real skulls buried in the dirt with just the few teeth left to grin up at the sun. Baby bodies dotting the dirt like bean sprouts in chow mein. I ain't afraid to look. Slant-eyed mommas crying over the limp remains of black haired sons. I seen it all. I seen it all. Let the crybabies stay home and hide in their moms' closets and wipe themselves with apple pie. No wars on foreign soils to quiver their weak little crotches. I don't want any one of them what's so tied up in a death struggle with his own dad that he can't go out and be a man and defend his home. I wouldn't want him in my platoon. Yes, boys. War is hell. And you have to be a hell of a man, with a hell of a lot of blood to spill for the hell of a lot of love you have for your hell of a country! Get aboard now and know that the U S A is behind you all the way. Ten thousand miles right here behind you. We'll show your dead brothers in arms that they did not die in vain. God love ya, and go get that guy, before he gets you first. For God. For country. For the land of the brave and the home of the free. Fall in!

(The men fall into single file led by the SERGEANT *and march in place as the female actors come on stage in concentrated force with rising sounds to form an airplane. The men march down and around the airplane, then halt.)*

SERGEANT: All right, ladies, prepare to go abroad. Next stop, Vietnam!

(The SERGEANT *supervises the men boarding the plane. The men enter, stand in middle of plane, attach their parachute cords, and face each other in two rows. The sound of the plane changes to one of take-off, the plane then levels off. The sound changes from that of an engine to one of spirits, high, but sweet. The plane arrives in Asia. The female actors melt away but stay concentrated. The men are left in a cluster on stage.)*

SERGEANT: All right, ladies, bail out!

(The men bail out one at a time. Some have to be pushed by the SERGEANT. *They yell, then count as they jump.)*

G IS: 1001, 1002, 1003, 1004, 1005, 1006.

(The chutes open, and they enjoy floating to earth. If the men move their feet very little, but feel the pull of gravity in their hips and thighs and steer the chutes with their arms, the effect can be quite touching.)

SERGEANT: *(Bails out and shouts)* Satchmo! Satchmo! Satchmo!

(The G IS *say their lines to the audience as they float down to earth.)*

G I ONE: I didn't prepare myself.

G I TWO: The clouds look like whipped potatoes.

G I THREE: That sergeant is as helpful as a bag full of holes.

G I FOUR: When I get home, I'm gonna make people stop and think.

G I FIVE: There, I'm getting my own individual style.

G I SIX: I wish Tuesday Weld could see me now.

G I SEVEN: When I catch her, I'm gonna kiss the daylights out of her.

G I EIGHT: This gives me tingles in my tummy.

G I ONE: I'd like to tell you that having been raised in a small and sheltered town, this is like going from one world into another.

G I TWO: Will I pass the test of life?

G I THREE: I can't wait to get there and make a killing in the black market.

G I FOUR: I'm making a career in the army because I just can't wait until the next day arrives so that I can see what interesting things are going to happen to me next.

G I FIVE: I joined the service to get some time to think.

G I SIX: Gee, it's a nice day.

G I SEVEN: John Wayne has faith in me.

G I EIGHT: Whores don't kiss.

G I ONE: I'm the greatest!

(The plane has overshot the Vietnam border and deposited our boys in Shangri-la. The SERGEANT *had landed beyond them. One of the actors quickly buries his chute, then climbs a bench to represent a mountain ridge, and assumes the carriage of the high* LAMA. *The other* G IS *pull down their chutes, quickly bury them, and when they see the high* LAMA *approach, they crouch with their guns drawn.)*

LAMA: *(Bowing)* Kama Sutra, Kemo Sabe! Siddartha has crossed the Rhine. Kissed the women and drinked the wine. The deep blue sea washes you and me. What is salt without stew? And the sound of one hand stealing is the shot heard around the world. While sojourning in our hidden paradise—enjoy, enjoy! Drink from our springs of happiness. Wash your G I socks in our fountain of foolishness. Become as little children and the Rat Race wrinkles will fade from your tongue.

(He bows and our boys bow back. Gong)

LAMA: You have arrived at the Holy Hiding Place of all our sons.

(He bows and our boys bow back. Gong)

LAMA: Allah has provided Buddha for all you sweet little white Jesuses. Feel free to rest in the arms of our mother bodies and trace your names on the breasts of time. Welcome to Shangri-la!

(The gong sounds. He bows to them and boys bow back. He goes back across to the bench and sits. As the last gong sounds the women enter as Shangri-la maidens. They sing in a high, sweet falsetto. The "yea yea" lines take to the audience.)

WOMEN: Welcome to Shangri-la.
Yea yea, welcome to Shangri-la yea yea.
Give us your Yankee Hand,
Jump into Love's quicksand,
Welcome to Shangri-la.
Yea yea.

Here you will drink of love,
Here you'll be raped by doves,
Welcome to Shangri-la.
Oh yea yea, welcome to Shangri-la
Shangri—Shangri—Yeah!

(They begin a slow-motion orgy with our boys.)

SERGEANT: *(Can be heard in the distance calling)* Alice Company? Alice Company? Alice Company? *(He spots the orgy.)* Aha! Aha! Aha! Aha! Aha! All right, you Little Bo Peeps! Ten-hut! Ten-hut! Ten-hut! I'll have you shot for AWOL. Let go a' the tits of human kindness and fall in! We got a job to do for our folks back home. Come on, you girls you, rise up. We have to get the freedom ringing. We can just make the jungle by the time the snow melts. Goddammit, you dogbodies! Pull up your pants and let's mush! Er, marsh. Forward. Mush.

G I ONE: Sir, just five more minutes!

SERGEANT: Ten-hut!

(The frightened platoon jumps to its feet. They straighten their clothes. The maidens follow, clinging to them. The maidens get in line behind the men.)

SERGEANT: Fall in! Ten-hut! Let's go, on the double. We have a job to do and we're not even at the right address yet.

(They start to march. The women learn the step quickly and all march in single file around the stage. As they march they burst into a marching song.)

To the jungle march
Through the jungle gore,
To the jungle march
Through the jungle roar.

We're off to fight for Vietnam,
We will display our might.
We're off to win for Vietnam,
We're fighting for what's fight.
To bring the girls of Vietnam
To be as free as we.

To make the boys of Vietnam
As free as the U S A.

To the jungle march
Through the jungle gore,
To the jungle march
Through the jungle roar.

(A wild frug can be interspersed with march. Or the march turns into a brief, high-spirited polka. Or the frug can be combined and choreographed and the ensemble can end in a lunatic war machine by the final stanza. They yell and step and kick. The dance ends. There is an immediate transformation and each person takes on the character he is to be first in the next scene. They crowd around one actor who seems to be preventing them from entering a room. They burst through, settle down, and we are in a Senate Investigating Committee room. The actors should take turns being senators and witnesses; the transformations should be abrupt and total. When the actor finishes with one character he becomes another, or just an actor. When not senators or witnesses they are the audience to the proceedings and take their places on benches to the side of the stage. They react in character to what transpires. There are reporters, photographers, etc. Everything must be pantomimed throughout the play.)

SENATOR ONE: *(Begins quickly)* I will make my opening remarks as brief as possible. The situation is grave, the perils immense. We hope with the aid of the Almighty to find a just, equitable, and profitable solution. May I call the first witness?

*(*WITNESS ONE *is in place facing the* SENATORS. *He has brought a chair from the sidelines to the center of the stage.)*

SENATOR TWO: *(To* WITNESS*)* Good morning, Sir.

WITNESS ONE: Good morning, Sir...er, Sirs.

SENATOR ONE: Do be seated, Sir.

WITNESS ONE: Thank you, Sir...er, Sirs. I am sitting.

SENATOR TWO: Sir, let me tell the people of America that we're very pleased to have a man of your caliber and illustrious career come forward to express his view on our position in...er...in...er...

*(*SENATOR ONE *whispers to him)*

SENATOR TWO: ...Vietnam

WITNESS ONE: I see it as my duty, Sir.

SENATOR ONE: Are you ready to express your views, Sir?

WITNESS ONE: Yes, sir...er, sirs... With all due respect to our Administration to whose commander and chief I am most loyal to, but sirs, it is time, I believe, that we stop pussy-footing around and won that war. From my vast experience in invading both islands and mainlands, with both foot soldiers and advanced weaponry, I say we have to lay our cards on the line and do the job. I say, get the atomic bulldozer operational. Get it off the drawing board and out bulling down that jungle. The native population should be moved temporarily to some valley in eastern California, and then get the hell the atomic bulldozer in there and push the jungle into the sea. That way there won't be any cover for the enemy to hide out in, we mop up, blacktop the cleared land—and then—shazam!—we have a hell of a parking lot for jet bombers for when the next domino threatens to fall.

SENATOR ONE: Well thought out.

WITNESS ONE: Someone had to do it, Sir.

SENATOR TWO: Next witness.

SENATOR ONE: You did it, Sir.

WITNESS ONE: Thank you, Sir.

SENATOR TWO: Next witness.

*(*WITNESS TWO, *grand old American Woman Statesman, starts to make her way to the witness chair. The* SENATORS *rush to help her settle herself, then they resume their seats. She looks around and smiles and tries to wave. Looks back at* SENATORS, *forgets what she's there for.)*

SENATOR TWO: An unexpected pleasure. How grand to see you again.

*(*WITNESS TWO *nods and smiles.)*

SENATOR ONE: Madam, the United States, as you know, is in a sort of a pickle. And we would relish your views on our position in Vietnam.

WITNESS TWO: People—of—America!

(Applause from spectators)

WITNESS TWO: When—Mr Thant—and—I—last—spoke—we were still saying—that—it—should be entrusted—to—the U N. How else can World—Law—take hold—to—People of America? I—implore you—to—support—the United Nations of the World....

(Applause. The two men who have been SENATORS *rush to the witness, pick her up, and carry her to her seat. As this happens two new* SENATORS *take the chairs.)*

SENATOR ONE: Thank you, thank you, thank you. That was most.... Next witness!

WITNESS THREE: *(A prize fighter takes the stand)* The greatest. That's me. Yeah, yeah, oh yeah. The greatest and the prettiest and the sweetest that you'll ever see. Yeah, yeah, oh yeah. Oh yeah.

SENATOR TWO: What is your position on our position in Vietnam?

WITNESS THREE: To a neutral corner you should retire, before all our pretty boys and cute tiny friends all expire.

SENATOR ONE: Will the witness please be clearer?

WITNESS THREE: My good name I will lend, your ear to bend. Two thousand X is my name.... Turn it around and it's still the same. Oh yeah. Yeah, yeah. Oh yeah.

SENATOR TWO: *(To* SENATOR ONE*)* A perfect specimen.

WITNESS THREE: Yeah, yeah, oh yeah. I'm the prettiest I'm the greatest, and I ratest with the girls. And to stay this way, I want to say; we got no quarrel with the northern race. And the place where I stand. And I'm grand. And I'm grand, man. Yeah, yeah, oh yeah. I am grand, man. Strike up the band.

SENATOR TWO: Next witness.

SENATOR ONE: We're grateful for your presence here today, sir. As a highly placed and trusted high-ranking high Government official and a high-ranking source of high information, state the latest official views, please.

WITNESS FOUR: Fellow officials...honored Senators, ladies and gentlemen of the press...my American fellows and gals, I want to tell you that this Administration to which I am a party to indulges in nothing but realism. I want to go on to say that realism does not rule out the hope that hope could come in the not too distant future... With calculated fluctuations, however...

SENATOR TWO: Sir, would you care to elaborate on However?

WITNESS FOUR: Why, Senator, I'd be glad to. If the ignorant and sensational press would just stop overreacting, we could get a job of hope really done around this globe. But no! Every tiny mistake, a few teensy bundles of bombs dropped in the wrong place, and the ignorant and sensational press just has to blow everything up. Blow it up. Blow it up. Blow it up. Bleep it. Blop. Bleep, gleep, blow. Sleep, sleep, sleep. Forgive me, but I haven't had any sleep in eighteen months. Blow it up. Blup. Blup.

(He falls into arms of usher who takes him to bench.)

WITNESS FIVE: *(A very neat and efficient man rushes to the stand.)* Senators, sirs, may I explain what my colleague meant....

SENATORS: We hope so.

WITNESS FIVE: *(He speaks quite rapidly like a mechanical man)* I want to assure you, sirs, and interested observers around the galaxy that we've begun to turn the tide. The moon is with us, we're not quite over the hump, but don't swallow the first deliberate propaganda line you see, but as free men learn to assess words. Words don't mean what they say. Actually the north is tactically defeated, but we haven't begun to see the end of this thing. Some of my colleagues are encouraged, some see a war of attrition, some are optimistic. And I'd like to say that for myself, I'm cautiously optimistic in my transistors and capacitors, but on certain days my entire circuit is in deep despair. There is a question that I'd like to put to you, Sirs?

SENATORS: Why, thank you, Sir. It's an honor.

WITNESS FIVE: Sirs: who is man?

SENATORS: Next witness!

WITNESS SIX: *(Rushes to take her place—a volatile, upset, intense woman)* I won't stop. I won't shut up. I will not keep quiet.

SENATOR TWO: Who's this?

SENATOR ONE: Not on the schedule.

WITNESS SIX: You must negotiate with all parties. Haven't you learned the lesson of assassination?

SENATORS: Assassination?

WITNESS SIX: You had my husband and brother-in-law killed and they had your President assassinated. In some circles that is called an eye for an eye, in others tit for tat.

SENATORS: This woman is in contempt. Arrest her!

WITNESS SIX: Hanoi is a beautiful city. I was born there. I want my children to see the streets where I walked as a girl. No one is safe! No one is safe.

(She rushes to a bench and seems to stab everyone sitting there. They slump over. She becomes only an actor again and takes her place on opposite bench. A moment of chaos.)

SENATOR TWO: Arrest. Order? Order? Order!

SENATOR ONE: Next witness.

*(*WITNESS SEVEN*, a curly-headed writer, slumps to the chair and sits on the back of it.)*

SENATOR TWO: It is indeed an honor to have a writer of your intense commitment take time off from his typewriter to give his views.

SENATOR ONE: What do you think we should do about the war in Vietnam?

WITNESS SEVEN: Nothing.

SENATOR TWO: Nothing?

WITNESS SEVEN: Nothing. The war will die of cancer. You'll die of cancer. Everyone will die of cancer. Me, I think too much. I'll die of cerebral hemorrhage.

SENATOR ONE: Nevertheless, as a leading writer of our country we'd be happy to hear if you possibly have a possible solution.

WITNESS SEVEN: The war ain't there, it's here. It's right here now, here and now. Mark those words carefully. I said mark them. That's all there is. That's what's happening, baby! It's here and now, here and now. You and me. Between you and me and me and me and you and and you and you and me and you and you and me. That's all that's happening, baby. Wise up before it's already happened to you. Check it out, baby, before they upchuck you—into oblivion, baby. The war ain't there, it's right here, here and now in this cancerous glare of the T V lights and tranquilized television dinners. Television, the tremendous masturbator of the masses. Vomit up the lard, you asses, before the future of our sperm is burned in Asiatic light. All you studs got to stop smearing napalm on the genitals of the weak. We got the fever. We don't got prosperity, we got the fever. Purge the bestial disease of the computer madness wigged into your shit by the bitch Goddess—burn out the blood of the malignant cells and cleanse your ego before it's too late. The horror from the sewer of our disease is rising up to choke your throat and all our images are manipulated from birth to death by cynics. Yeah boys, get out there and bomb the bomb before you die of cancer or you'll eat the fire next time! Madness leaped up! Madness leaped up and stomped on our hearts. Into oblivion baby.

(He is dragged to a bench by two ushers.)

SENATOR ONE: Next witness!

*(*WITNESS EIGHT *is an Indian who does a controlled but violent dance to the witness chair, chanting a Peyote Song.)*

SENATOR TWO: I beg your pardon?

WITNESS EIGHT *(After pause)* Song of my people.

SENATOR TWO: Can you give the nation, your nation's view of the situation in Vietnam?

WITNESS EIGHT: *(After a long pause, a shadow of a smile. He gathers himself up and, shaking from within, fires at them.)* This is the end of the line for you—and all you white men. The red man and the yellow man and the black man are banding together. We will run you off the scorched face of this earth. We will run you into the sea. We will fly you into the air. Your turn to sing now, white man. *(He starts for his place on the bench slowly, looking at the* SENATORS, *with each phrase.)* Goodbye, white man. White man! White man!

*(*WITNESS NINE, *several Vietnamese women, crying softly, go to kneel before the* SENATORS. *They plead and cry. Their hands flutter in bewilderment.)*

SENATOR TWO: What have we here, Senator?

SENATOR ONE: They're Vietnamese. Thought it only democratic we ask the opinion of the common people over there.

SENATOR TWO: Good man, Senator, good man.

*(*WITNESSES' *crying mounts. The* SENATORS *try to pacify them.)*

SENATOR ONE: Hush now.

SENATORS *(Uncomfortably)* It won't have been in vain. We promise you.

SENATOR ONE: Your men have not died in vain.

SENATOR TWO: Wait'll you see the swell schools and the great highways and turnpikes we're going to build in your jungle.

SENATOR ONE: It won't be a jungle any more.

SENATOR TWO: Why, why you know what we'll do to make it up to you? We'll turn the whole Mekong Delta into another T V A!

SENATOR ONE: What do you think about that?

(They cry louder. The SENATOR *rises and gestures.)*

SENATOR ONE: Er, Usher! Usher, will you please escort these ladies to the powder room. I think they want to freshen up.

(The WITNESSES *rise and quietly resume their seats. A beautiful woman,* WITNESS TEN *has taken her place in the witness chair. She arranges herself and maintains a radiant pose. The* SENATORS *rise in an attitude of prayer. Those on the benches kneel in place. Some sing, and others chant. The* SENATORS *move to the seated woman, genuflect, and place some small coins in her open palm. They genuflect again and back toward their chairs.)*

SENATOR ONE: Madonna, words cannot express the pleasure we feel in your presence.

SENATORTWO: Madonna, what is your position on Vietnam?

(The MADONNA *carefully and slowly strikes and holds another pose. The actress playing this role should study famous paintings and sculptures of the Madonna and Child. She should choose four that suit her and that are clear to the audience. The* SENATORS *ask her three more times to state her position on Vietnam.)*

SENATOR ONE: *(Chanting)* Holy Mother, we thank you for your views.

(The MADONNA, *gracefully and maintaining a pose, exits to her place on the bench, but it would be nice if she flew straight up and out of sight.)*

SENATOR TWO: Next witness!

*(*WITNESS ELEVEN, *a serene faced, beautiful man approaches. He makes a sign and steps over the chair and continues to benches on other side of stage and makes a sign of blessing.)*

WITNESS ELEVEN: Bless you. Bless you Bless you.

SENATOR TWO: What is your statement, sir?

WITNESS ELEVEN: Love, brother.

SENATOR ONE: *(Who should be a woman by now)* Love?

WITNESS ELEVEN: Love, sister.

SENATOR ONE: Did you say Love?

WITNESS ELEVEN: Love, daughter.

SENATOR ONE: Love...?

WITNESS ELEVEN: Love...Mother.

SENATOR ONE: *(Approaches the* WITNESS *with a hypnotized smile)* Love?

WITNESS ELEVEN: Love.

SENATOR ONE: *(Gently touching the heart of the* WITNESS*)* Yeah, Love.

WITNESS ELEVEN: If you do not love—father and I will walk away. You're on your own. Love. Love or perish.

(He leaves and walks upstage where he stands with his back to the audience. Other people in the room begin to kiss, shake hands, sit with their arms around each other. Everyone becomes engaged in overt loving. One couple sends love out to the audience.)

SENATOR ONE: *(In a daze, walks back to her chair)* Love. *(She kisses* SENATOR TWO.*)*

WITNESS TWELVE: *(A vigorous contemporary patriot jumps up and runs to the witness chair)* What is this soft-headed, lily-livered kind of thinking? Is this for patriots? Love can't stop criminals or tyrants. Love is no good without a body to express it. Get out there and defend the right to happiness of our brothers. *(He leaps up on the chair.)* We went across the Atlantic to fight for freedom. Are you frightened to cross the Pacific?

CROWD: *(Reacts)* No, no!

WITNESS TWELVE: The world has shrunk to the size of a pea. We are our brother's keeper. The flag of the United States of America shall shelter all who wish our aid. Hold your tongue. Stiffen your spine. There is still something worth fighting and worth dying for. The same thing our fathers and grandfathers fought and died for at Valley Forge, Gettysburg, the Alamo, Anzio, Guadalcanal, Iwo Jima, Okinawa, Pork Chop Hill.

(The crowd is all around his chair now.)

WITNESS TWELVE: Freedom. Let freedom ring! Kill for freedom!

(The crowd repeats. He starts to sing America the Beautiful. *Everyone sings with genuine patriotic fervor. They hoist him on their shoulders. They march all over the committee room. They march straight toward the audience, stop short, do an about-face. Salute, hold hands on hearts, etc for one full chorus, then march out on the second one. They should sing with all the genuine love and gusto they can muster. Big, big, big)*

END OF ACT ONE

ACT TWO

(Open with the stage filled by all the actors; it should have the feeling of irregular squares. Some face audience. Some face stage left, others stage right. Some face upstage. They sing "America" exuberantly as before, but no sound comes out. [If a proscenium stage is used, begin a Rockette chorus line and kick all the way to stage front.] Every two lines they do an exact about-face so that they are facing opposite direction from opening of act. When they reach the chorus, they march to the formation for the next scene. Then all but three people fall to their knees and take up positions facing audience. Left standing are one G I, *a* MOTHER, *a* GIRL. *They are in the center of the mass of bodies in a triangle facing outward. The women who play "sweethearts" throughout the play kneel in front of the* GIRL. *Women who play "mothers" throughout the play kneel in front of* MOTHER. *Boys kneel in front of* G I. *As the scene begins all the actors on the floor should flirt with the audience, using only their eyes. It should be the effect of group snapshots in which only the eyes move. However, the three principals are mobile. As the scene progresses the three may change places. The scene should end with them clustered together, arms and bodies closely intertwined, but their faces still toward audience.)*

G I: March 9, 1966, My Tho, Vietnam. Dear Mother... My dear baby Janet...

MOTHER: March 9, 1966, Kittitas City, Washington. My dearest beloved son...

GIRL: March 9, 1966, Kittitas City, Washington. Hi, darlin! Hi, honey! Hello, my lemon-drop kid! Boy, Eugene, am...

G I: Hi, Mom. I'm staying warm. The sun here's about two thousand degrees. My feet are still coal black from...

MOTHER: I wish I could be making you some chicken and dumplings. They called me from...

GIRL: I'm counting the days till your tour of duty is up. How's the sightseeing in the rice paddies?

MOTHER: ...the Washington Chapter of American Mothers and told me I'd been chosen our state's Mother of the Year. O K, now have a good laugh.

G I: ...being wet and walking in the rice paddies, but on Sunday, I'm going to bleach them out with lemon like you suggested. Janet, baby, I can't stop thinking about that Goulet record. War is terrible, honey, but one thing it sure as hell teaches you is what it...

MOTHER: I guess I do feel proud, but I hate to think that one of the reasons they're making me Mother of the Year is because you are fighting for our country so far away on a foreign shore.

GIRL: ...Boy, I know I'm supposed to cheer you up when I write you and all, but the television news scares you know what right out of me, honey. I know you have to fight for freedom, but honey, please don't go out of your way...

G I: is that is important in life. And you are it for me. Mom, I'm so glad you're managing to keep busy and all.

MOTHER: ...The farm is...doing fine, but I have to tell you I've had to lease out most of it. But I kept the piece of land where you rigged the swimming hole in the irrigation ditch....

GIRL: ...I ache for you. I love your letters. I've got them all near memorized....

G I: You wouldn't believe how being tired and away from home and loved ones can knock you out....

GIRL: By the time you get home, I just know I'll have enough in savings for our down payment. Our house. Just us.

MOTHER: I'd give my right arm, if I could just hear your voice on the phone. But I'm placing my trust in God, and in your good sense.

G I: Well, Mom, I have to hit the sack.

GIRL: I got all the furniture all picked out for the master bedroom.

MOTHER: Got to find something to wear when they pin that corsage on me. Hope it isn't gardenias.

G I: Keep the letters coming, honey. They mean a lot. I'm putting on weight, Mom.

GIRL: I want you. I'll write you again before I go to bed.

MOTHER: I love you with all my heart.

G I: ...Your loving son, Eugene.

GIRL: Oh, Eugene, Eugene, my Eugene... Your own little girl, Janet.

MOTHER: Come home just as soon as you can; all my love, dearest son, Your Mom.

G I: Stay by me, Janet. I'll be home soon. All my love, Eugene...

(By now the three have locked arms in a circle and keep turning while saying their last sentences. This should repeat until all actors are standing. With the closing lines, all actors should rise and march their counterpart to the next formation. All girls go to back wall or side wall to become male South Vietnamese soldiers. The men march around stage to the shouts of their SERGEANT. *The girls assemble themselves in an extraordinarily ragged and unruly line. They are now South*

Vietnamese soldiers. They make their lunches as they wait in the hot sun. They entertain themselves by singing sentimental love songs. Each actress should sing her favorite secret love song. All this should go on at the same time. One definitely should sing Someone to Watch Over Me.*)*

SERGEANT: *(To men)* Halt! At ease, girlie burgers.

G IS: You said it. We been on the steam table nine days long.

SERGEANT: *(Gesturing to girls)* Meet your comrades in arms. These here are our allies and your counterparts. The ARVN troops. These here is the South Vietnamese men you're going to teach to fight like American soldiers.

G IS: They're awful little.

SERGEANT: But big enough to pull a trigger.

G I ONE: They's so purty, they look like girls.

SERGEANT: These is your new buddies. You are here to train them to be like you.

G I TWO: I don't trust girls.

SERGEANT: These are South Vietnamese troops. And you are girls.

G I THREE: But, but, Sergeant—

SERGEANT: Dry up, Esmeralda!

G I FOUR: They ain't big enough to carry a gun.

SERGEANT: You'll teach 'em. They'll learn to shoot, but just be sure the guns ain't pointed at you.

G IS: *(Laughing)* Get him. Gee whiz, Sarge, you're always joking us.

SERGEANT: You keep your eyes swiveled.

G I FIVE: Sergeant, what do the Viet Cong look like?

SERGEANT: *(Pointing to girls)* Like them.

G I SIX: How do we know who to shoot at?

SERGEANT: You shoot by ear, boobie. If you hear someone shoot at you, you shoot back.

G IS: Yes, sir.

SERGEANT: You better believe it! Live by your ears, Alice, and you might grow up to be Elizabeth.

G I THREE: You said I was Elizabeth.

SERGEANT: That was yesterday. Today is today. And don't you forget it, Maude!

G IS: *(Saluting)* Yes, siree...Mother...

SERGEANT: Now get out there and win those guys' hearts and win those guys' minds, or we'll never get those guys' trigger fingers on our guys' side.

G I SEVEN: Can they talk American?

SERGEANT: Teach 'em. What's the matter with you shitheads—are you ladies or are you girls?

G IS: *(Shouting)* Ladies!

SERGEANT: *(Yelling back)* Gung Ho—satchmo!

G IS: *(Yelling back)* Right away!

(The SERGEANT *stalks off. The* G IS *gingerly and shyly kick the dirt all the way to where the Vietnamese sit, eating and humming. They try to get their attention.)*

JERRY: *(Taking the situation in hand)* Hi there! How ya doing? Way to go. Thata boy. What a' ya say?

ARVIN: I like you—you number one big shot of the world.

JERRY: Hey, that's pretty good. Ain't it, boys?

G IS: That's pretty good. But do they know any Rock?

JERRY: *(Squatting by the girls)* Me Yankee.

ARVIN: *(Repeating after him)* Me Yankee.

JERRY: Yeah, hey hey, that's pretty good. Ain't it, boys?

G IS: Yeah, pretty good. Way to go.

JERRY: Me Yankee, you dickhead.

ARVIN: *(Repeating)* Me Yankee, you dickhead.

JERRY: Well now, that's pretty good, but it's *(He gestures to himself and then to them.)* Me, Me, Me, Jerry, Me Yankee, you, you, you South Vietnamese, you dickhead.

ARVIN: *(Nodding happily)* Oooooooooooooooo. We get. We dickhead, you Yankee.

JERRY: *(Pleased with himself)* That's right, that's right. *(Points to his head)* Head.

*(*ARVIN *repeats in Oriental-French accent.)*

JERRY: Nose, clothes, arms, hand. Finger. Trigger finger. *(They hold up trigger fingers.)*

G IS: Come on, Jerry. Ask them where the girls are.

JERRY: Shut up, you guys. Don'tcha know, there's a war on? *(Back to* ARVIN*)* Boot. One boot. Two boot.

ARVIN: *(Likes the sound of that. They start singing.)* One boot. One boot. One boot loved two boot.

JERRY: That's good. That's good. Gee, these guys learn fast.

G IS: Yeah, but don't they know any Rock?

JERRY: *(To* ARVIN*)* Only one thing, you cute little guys. One thing. Don't shoot the boot. No no no. Don't shoot the boot.

ARVIN: No no no. We no shoot the boot. Love boot.

JERRY: No shoot the boot boot. Shoot the head, or shoot heart heart. No shoot the boot boot. Shoot the heart.

ARVIN: No no shoot heart. Love in heart.

JERRY: *(Getting mad)* Come on, you guys. There's a war going on here. You got to shoot the enemy's heart. Come on, you guys.

ARVIN: Oooooooooooooooo we get. No shoot the boot boot. Shoot the heart heart.

JERRY: That's right, way to go. Good show. Gee, these guys are pretty damn smart. Look how fast they learn. *(To his men)* Hey, you guys, aren't these little guys smart?

G IS: Gee, they're smarter than we thought. Ask them where the girls are.

JERRY: *(Gives his men a tough look. Back to* ARVIN*)* Gee, you guys are awfully cute. Maybe I'll take back one for Mom. You appeal to my American heart.

ARVIN: Shoot the heart heart.

JERRY: That's right, that's right, but not mine. The Viet Cong. The enemy. You know the enemy. We call him Victor Charlie, that's code. The other guy. You know, get out there and get that guy and shoot him in his heart heart. Me—I'm your Yankee teacher.

ARVIN: You bet your boot boot.

JERRY: Gee, you guys have a way of catching on.

G IS: Hey, Jerry, ask them where the girls are.

JERRY: *(To men)* Get me an M-18!

(They do so.)

JERRY: This is my big gun. *(He picks out a girl.)* This is your best friend. Hey, you, you there, come out here.

(She comes out shyly.)

JERRY: Hold the gun.

(She does.)

JERRY: Now, tell me about the gun.

MURIEL: Boot.

JERRY: No no no boot. That is gun.

MURIEL: Gun.

JERRY: Yeah, gun. Tell me about it.

MURIEL: *(Looks at her friends, they gesture to her)* Gun. Gun heavy.

JERRY: That's right. What else?

MURIEL: Gun heavy. Gun greasy.

JERRY: That's right What else?

(MURIEL shrugs her shoulders.)

JERRY: This gun is an instrument. What can you do with this instrument?

MURIEL: This gun is heavy, greasy instrument. *(She pauses, looks at her friends, then she goes into wild Dixieland pose and puts the gun barrel to her mouth as if it were a trumpet.)* And I'm a gonna blow it....

(Fast chorus of The Saints Go Marching In *and her friends join in. Chaos)*

JERRY: *(Restoring order)* Hey, you guys, ten-hut! Ten-hut! *(He gestures to his comrades.)* Issue them M-18's with fixed bayonets. Now you guys, follow me. Do what I do. Chop chop. Kill kill. That's the way.

(G Is go through attack-and-kill pantomime while singing the following song.)

JERRY: What's the spirit of the bayonet?

ROY: The spirit of the bayonet is....

G IS: Kill kill kill.

JERRY: The spirit of the bayonet?

ALL: Kill kill kill.

JERRY: Chop chop.

ROY: Kill kill.

JERRY: Warm blood chop.

ROY: Warm blood kill.

JERRY: The spirit of the bayonet?

ALL: Kill kill kill.

ROY: The spirit of the bayonet?

ALL: Kill kill kill.
Chop chop
Kill kill
Chop chop
Kill kill
The spirit of the bayonet
Chop spirit chop
Kill blood kill

Chop spirit chop
Kill blood kill
The spirit of the bayonet
Kill Kill Kill!

JERRY: *(Addresses this to the audience)* Now, we're off on a war game. This is just pretend, see. We're going out to look for V-C. We're going to flush him out and then we're going to engage him, and then we're going to kill that guy. But this first time, it's just pretend, see? Pretend. *(He makes a shush with his finger and his eyes twinkle. Back to the troops)* Now you new guys get in back of these seasoned troops here.

(He gestures to his men, who line up in front of the girls.)

JERRY: O K, everybody. All together now. Sound off!

(They count cadence. At shout of four, the ARVIN *turn into Viet Cong and stab our boys in the back with the bayonets. The men fall. The women pick over their bodies looking for weapons to steal. Then all but two run and hide.)*

SERGEANT: *(Comes stalking on)* All right, you guys. Let's shape up to ship out. *(He stops cold when he sees the scene of destruction. His nose runs.)* What's this? What's this? My little girls. My boys, my men. What the shit happened to my men?

(Two girls are left. One of them pretends to be hurt. The other holds her. They look at him and say:)

ARVIN: Sorry about that.

SERGEANT: It's all my fault. They was still wet behind the ears. I shouldn't've left 'em alone. Which way did the bastards go? V-C? You see V-C?

(The girls nod.)

SERGEANT: Which way...which way?

(The girls point in all directions.)

SERGEANT: I'll get me a bag of new recruits. I'll run down them V-C's and rub their noses in it. *(Addressing the audience)* I wish the people back home could see this sight. They wouldn't have any question any more of why we is here. Look at my ladies. I nursed 'em through boot and stopped the airsickness. I taught them how to kill. You're never ready for death. Never. I seen it over and over. Young men, never ready for death. Not one is. Never. I would like to take every one of those bleeding-heart liberals and make him put each one of our dead boys in the green bag death sack. I would like to see those baldheaded, wet-mouthed liberals up to their balls in the blood of our boys and how they could take loading these sweet lost bodies into the death-copter. I'd give both arms for one sight like that. Those sons-of-bitching V-C are going to pay for the lives of my guys, even if I personally have to hunt down and skin each and every one of them. You'll see me again. You can bet your ass on that!

(The girls run off with their weapons and hide. The SERGEANT *executes a complete about-face in place. He treats the fallen men as if they're sleeping in their sacks. He wakes them from a deep sleep.)*

SERGEANT: All right, boobies. Up and at 'em. Get the lead out. Get out of that sack. Ship up your shapes. I just lost my crack squad to the dirty sneaky charlies, and you're going out to get even with them if it's the last thing you ever do. And it may be. Get me? Wipe the snot off your nose, droopy drawers. Smarten up and fly right. You're going to shape up so fast you won't have time to shit.

G IS: Yes, sir. Yes, siree, Mother!

SERGEANT: Forward march.

(The men march forward and walk square into the wall. They fall. Then they turn on their bellies and crawl across an open rice paddy as the mortars go off and sniper bullets zing by. One by one they raise their heads and address the audience.)

G I ONE: When I was a little boy I used to eat a spoonful of dirt every day.

G I TWO: Similar things are not identical.

G I THREE: I seem to have a lot of ground to cover.

G I FOUR: Six percent of the world's population controls sixty percent of its wealth.

G I FIVE: Hello,young lovers.

G I SIX: Green Mint Formula 47 gives you confidence about your mouth.

G I SEVEN: When I get home I'm gonna run for Congress.

G I EIGHT: Have you been paid this week?

G I ONE: Its all right to be angry. It's all right.

G I TWO: They laughed when I stood up to shoot.

G I THREE: I thought you were going to phone me?

G I FOUR: Go down Moses, Jack, Jim, and Sally.

G I FIVE: I dreamed I saw J F K last night alive as you and me.

G I SIX: "Nothing is worth my life."

G I SEVEN: For the last seven years we've been sending children through college.

G I EIGHT: God love you.

G I ONE: You have the smile of an angel. An angel.

(A mortar explodes. They dive for cover. JERRY *is hurt. He moans and screams. The men crawl to him and try to administer to his wounds. The* SERGEANT *sends over his walkie-talkie for the helicopter. The men lift* JERRY *and move slowly in a*

circle as if in a helicopter. Then they place him alone on floor of stage. All go to the benches to be ready for the next scene. JERRY *is alone lying on the stage; he pulls his shirt over his face. One steps forward and sings.)*

SINGER: Please God, I ask not for myself.
Please God, bring him home safe.
Please God, he has a heart of gold.
Please God, watch over his life,
He has only six more months to go.

(A family sits together on a bench to one side of the stage. An OFFICER *appears and knocks.)*

OFFICER: Mr Small?

FATHER: Yes?

OFFICER: I'm Captain Statzz. I'm to accompany your wife to Vietnam.

FATHER: Yes, of course. She'll be ready in a minute.

(He goes to his wife, and she shakes her head. They freeze.)

SINGER: *(Sings to music of* Please God*)*
His mother waits to see his face,
To press the beat of his heart of gold.
Please God, bring him home safe,
Our family Marine with stance so bold,
He has only six more months to go.

MOTHER: No. You go.

FATHER: Dear. You're the only one allowed.

MOTHER: I can't stand it.

FATHER: You've got to.

MOTHER:Yes.

(They freeze.)

SINGER: *(Sings)* Please God, it's not too late.
Please God, his family prays.
Please God, his loved ones wait.
Please God, he's only nineteen,
He has only six more months to go.

*(*CAPTAIN *turns and changes into* PILOT. MRS SMALL *kisses her husband goodbye and follows* PILOT.*)*

PILOT: This way, Mrs Small. Fasten your seat belt.

MOTHER: Sir, why can't my husband go too? After all, he's Jerry's father.

PILOT: We only have seats for mothers.

MOTHER: All the rest of these seats...?

PILOT: ...will be occupied by mothers.

(Plane takes off. The MOTHER *holds a baby in her arms, reminiscent of one of the poses of the* MADONNA *in ACT ONE.)*

SINGER: *(Sings)* His mother longs to see his face,
To press the beat of his heart of gold.
Please God,
Please God,
Please God,
He has only six more months to go.

*(*SINGER *retires to the bench. Plane lands.* PILOT *changes into* DOCTOR. *They walk to entrance of field hospital.)*

MOTHER: Is he here?

DOCTOR: Down this corridor, Mrs Small.

MOTHER: Are you sure you've done....

DOCTOR: All we know how.

MOTHER: How long, Doctor, how long do I...does he have?

DOCTOR: I'm sure you'll have at least two hours.

MOTHER: Doctor?

DOCTOR: Yes?

MOTHER: Will he know me?

DOCTOR: You're his mother.

MOTHER: I'm his mother.

DOCTOR: Your son is tagged.

MOTHER: Tagged?

DOCTOR: Name, rank, and serial number on a tag at his wrist.

MOTHER: Will I know him?

DOCTOR: His voice—you'll know his voice.

MOTHER: You'll go with me?

DOCTOR: Mrs Small, I'd like to, but I have many boys to save.

MOTHER: I can't do it.

DOCTOR: Mrs Small, we're sorry about this.

MOTHER: Please come with me.

DOCTOR: I'm needed.

MOTHER: I don't know where to start.

DOCTOR: He should be the third man in.

(She starts down the path of boys. She finds hers and bends to read the tag.)

MOTHER: Gerald...Gerald Rogers Small, Sp. 2nd Class, Company 107. Gerald Rogers Small. Gerald Rogers? Doctor...Doctor... It's a mistake. It's all a mistake...a grave mistake.

DOCTOR: *(Running in)* Mrs Small...please, men are....

MOTHER: The tag. Doctor, the tag...

DOCTOR: Let's see.

MOTHER: A mistake. This says Gerald Rogers Small.

DOCTOR: So it does.

MOTHER: You see, it's all a mistake. My son's middle name isn't Rogers, it's Robert. Gerald Robert Small. Robert. Robert!

JERRY: *(Moaning)* Momma...charming Jerry...Momma...charming Jerry

MOTHER: *(A chill goes through her as she recognizes her son's voice)* Jerry...?

DOCTOR: *(Quietly)* Typist made the error, Mrs Small. Sorry about that. *(He leaves.)*

MOTHER: Jerry.

JERRY: Momma...Momma?

*(*JERRY *dies. The* MOTHER *mourns. Abrupt transformation into a Buddhist funeral. The sound becomes Vietnamese. The scene transforms immediately from that of the army field hospital to a Vietnamese hamlet. The American* MOTHER *becomes the Vietnamese* MOTHER, *and* JERRY *becomes her dead son. All the other actors participate as villagers and mourners. The Buddhist* PRIEST *rises and presides over the group. His shoulders are tense, his eyes half-closed, and his voice has many tones and slides. The speech should be on tape but also should be said by the actor, sometimes synchronized, sometimes a little ahead of the tape, sometimes a bit behind the tape, but ending in synchronization.)*

PRIEST: *(Burning incense in containers in both hands, he waves the incense as he bends and weaves in a slow-motion dance at foot of the body.)* Whatever spirits have come together here, either belonging to the earth or living in the air, let us worship the perfect Buddha, revered by gods and men; may there be salvation. Whatever spirits have come together here, either belonging to the earth or living in the air, let us worship the perfect Dharma, revered by gods and men; may there be salvation. Whatever spirits have come together here, either belonging to the earth or living in the air, let us worship the perfect Sangha, revered by gods and men; may there be salvation.

(He looks toward the body and directs the next lines to the body and also to the congregation. All mourn.)

PRIEST: A Buddha is the embodiment of Dharma, which is his real body. He is identified with all the constituents of the universe. This body is invisible and universal. All beings "live and move and have their being in it."

(Brief mourning and crying, then a man rises and sings to audience.)

SETH: *(Rises in a spotlight to sing alone to the audience)*
Don't put all your eggs in one basket.
Baskets wear out and men die young.
Better to marry trees or elephants.
Men die young,
Some cities survive.
Go and pick yourself one
Because men die young, my dear,
Because men die young.

Don't put all your eggs in one basket.
Find several to keep
In reserve, my dear.
Men die young.

Since men are dying younger every year,
Be careful what you choose
Or you'll be alone the next twenty years.
Because men die young, my dear,
Because men die young.

You don't want to lose
The chance to cover your bets,
So love as much as you can, my dear,
Because men die young

Try all available delicacies,
Don't concentrate on only one,
Because men die young, my dear,
Because men die young.

Some cities survive,
Go and pick yourself one, Because men die young, my dear,
Because men die young.

(All actors get into place for next scene, all the women except the one who is to play HANOI HANNAH *rush out into the audience as spotlights pick out various sections of the house. Each woman chooses a section and delivers the same speech.)*

WOMEN: This war is worms. This war is worms invaded by worms. This war is eating away at the boy flesh inside my belly. This war stinks. This war takes men away and pins back the man in me so he can't kick and scream, which is his God-given right. This war stinks. This war makes everybody more warlike than they are anyway. This war invades me and makes me hate myself. I hate you. I hate you. And you—I hate you! *(Quieter)* This war is wounds. This war is worms.

(Women take their places on bench at back on stage. The men, led by SERGEANT, *crawl in and dig in for a siege. Much sound of mortar and gunfire. Then sudden stillness. The men are dug in. There is a lull. it's dark. They semi-relax and listen. Each may react to* HANNAH*'s lines according to his character. Some make fun of her archaic English terms. The audience should hear what they say. A crazy Chinese soap-opera organ plays under her speech. She sits in chair to one side of stage and reads from copy over mike.)*

HANOI HANNAH: Good evening, my little baby ball, Yankee imperialists. How goes our tiny battle today? This is your bosom buddy and wishful lover, Hanoi Hannah, bringing you the truth from around the world. I'm here to keep you warm for your sweetheart back home. Float to your lover on my voice. See her sweet body and the nape of her dear neck after you have nuzzled her in the back seat of your roadster. Feel her pulsating to your eager hands under her shift as you undress her on the back seat of your touring car. Feel her rush to meet your passion, guiding the most exciting part of you into the most exciting part of her. Smell the pungent love you share. Do you not savor that moment again as you lie in your imperialistic criminal foxholes? You who bring murderous destruction to a people who fight only for their own homes. Where is your sweetheart now, my dear little baby ball G Is? She is in the arms of a new man back home, while you fight here in a foreign land. She is in the back seat of a 1966 roadster, with somebody else. And now *he* is removing her shift and plunging into your property. How does that make you feel, G I? Does that make you want to fight for what is yours? Do so, my little imperialistic lovers, but do so in your own back-yard. *(She plays a short Asian version of* Back in Your Own Back Yard. *Marching music softly under the next speech)* It's me again, your Indo-China lover, Hanoi Hannah, back again for our educational talk, my tiny round-eyed G I. You must understand that everything is divisible—specially the colossus of the United States, especially the immoral giant of U S imperialism. It will be and should be split up and defeated. The people of Asia, Africa, and Latin America can destroy the United States piece by piece, some striking at its head and others at its feet... You are too spread out, my tiny G Is. You cannot be every place at once. You cannot be here in Vietnam and also guard your Stateside sweetheart and your Momma too. And what of your dollars, your Yankee dollars, tiny round-eyed G I!? Who is making all those dollars, while you fight here in mud and are sucked by leeches and get only army pay? Everything is divisible, my tiny G I! Your head may be divided from your trunk, your arm from your shoulder, your heart from your head, your sex from your soul. Pull yourself together and confess to the world that you were wrong. Victory will go to the people of the world! It is inevitable. Long live the victory of the people's war!

(Soft music again for the next speech)

HANOI HANNAH: This is your wishful lover and bosom buddy, Hanoi Hannah, saying, sweet dreams in your hole, but I wouldn't close an eye; you may never open it again, tiny round-eyed G I. Good night, my bad little boys. I'll be with you again this time tomorrow night without a shift on... Sweet nightmare and... Aloha... *(She plays a crazy lullaby by an Asian jazz band.)*

(The men battle the V-C for an instant. Silence again and one of the boys takes out his guitar. The men lie in a bomb crater and come in on But I'm Too Far from Home.*)*

JERRY: I want a chocolate soda.
I want a Cracker Jack.

I want a little baby
To scratch my aching back.
I want my little baby
To scratch my aching back.

But I'm too far from home

(Men join in.)

I traveled hot and dusty
And sweated all my pores.
I traveled hot and dusty,
My feets all fulla sores.

I want my little baby
To scratch my aching back.

But I'm too far from home

(Men join in.)

I beat me down a jungle
And shot myself a man.
I beat me down a jungle
And shot myself a man.

Gimme my little baby
To scratch my aching back.

But I'm too far from home

(Men join in.)

I got my rocket-launcher.
I got my M-18.
I got my rainslick poncho.
Got my *Playboy* magazine.
But I—

Want my little baby
To scratch my aching back.

But I'm too far from home

(Men join in.)

(All but two men crouch down and begin to crawl across stage as if moving through high grass.)

(A G I *waves to audience alone at end of song.)*

JOE: Hi, folks. I want to tell you how proud I am to be able to be in direct contact with such fine and sunny-eyed supporters as you great American people. I need that support, and I tell you it feels good where it is most needed, in my head and hands and heart. I'll fight for you. I'll fight for you guys any day of the week. You're good people. The best!

[Cue for alternate scene]

(The SERGEANT *pulls him down.)*

(A G I *addresses the audience alone.)*

FRED: Sometimes you have to do things that you wouldn't ordinarily choose to do because you happen to be born in the greatest country in the world. What if I'd been born in the underside of a African tree, the daughter of a Pygmy witch doctor? I'm proud to serve and to save the people at home from having to fight on their very own doorsteps. I'll stay halfway around the world to see that our commitments are kept so my mom can get her milk on our front porch every morning without my mom having to duck the bullets. No, sir!

(The SERGEANT *pulls him to ground and he starts crawling.)*

ROY: *(Crawling and alternately resting)* Next battle, next battle I'm gonna get up on the high ground and put a bullet through the back of the sergeant's neck.

PAUL: *(Crawling and alternately resting)* I don't care. I don't give a shit. I don't care. I can't...nothing...big zero.

ROY: If I can just get high enough, the bullet will come out at the base of his collar in front and they'll never know.

PAUL: I wouldn't give a shit if the whole planet melted into lava and made red candy hearts across the universe. I don't care. I'm not even angry... I don't care.

ROY: I'll get up in a high Vietnamese tree and next contact with the enemy I'll get him in the back of the neck. And then I'll stay there.

SETH: Do you know where I can buy a greeting card for a guy who's been blown up by a mine?

SERGEANT: Ten-hut. You've earned it, ladies—three-day leave in Saigon.

(They march off, singing.)

G Is: Let's get to Saigon
And blitz the bars.
We'll load up on booze
Till we see stars.

Gonna get me a slant-eye
In old Saigon.
She'll feed me booze
And I'll make her a son.

We'll shack up tight
In her hootchie-cootch
And love all night
To the goonie-gootch.

Let's get to Saigon
And blitz the bars.
We'll load up on booze
Till we see stars.

Till we see stars
In her hootchie-cootch
And love all night
To the goonie-gootch.

Till we see stars!
Till we see stars!
Till we see stars.
Till we see stars...

[pick up here at end of alternate scene]

(The stage is filled with dancing bodies. SAIGON SALLY *sings in her bar and leads the dance. Two others join her in song.)*

SAIGON SALLY: Anti-hero baby
Anti-hero baby
Anti-hero baby
Anti-hero baby
Baby, baby,
Hero baby mine

Anti-hero baby
Anti-hero baby
Anti-hero baby
Anti-hero baby
Baby, baby,
Hero baby mine

Anti-hero baby
Anti-hero baby
Anti-hero baby
Anti-hero baby
Baby, baby,
Hero baby mine

Anti-hero baby
Anti-hero baby
Anti-hero baby
Anti-hero baby
Baby, baby,
Hero baby mine

Anti-hero baby
Anti-hero baby
Anti-hero baby
Anti-hero baby
Baby, baby,
Hero baby mine

Anti-hero baby
Anti-hero baby
Anti-hero baby
Anti-hero baby
Baby, baby,
Hero baby mine

(As the dance ends an exuberant G I *shouts a toast. The* SERGEANT *drinks at the bar. Couples pair off and slower dancing begins.)*

G I: Here's to Saigon Sally! She runs the swingingest bar in all of 'Nam!

SALLY: Sure I do, baby. You and me and L B J.

G I: *(Toasting)* Barbecue today with L B J.

(As the toast sinks in the SERGEANT*'s clouded brain, he begins to smolder. He whips around and tries to see which one of his men is shouting.)*

G I: Let's all go gay for L B J.

G I: I lost my way with L B J.

G I: March to doomsday with L B J.

G I: I lost my green beret on the Road to Mandalay.

ALL: *(Singing)* Glory, Glory, what a hell of a way to die.

G I: I got syphilis today, courtesy L B J.

ALL: *(Singing)* Glory, Glory, what a hell of a way to die! ...And we never shot a goddam Cong!

SERGEANT: *(Bulldozing his way into the men and breaking them up)* Knock it off, you boozed-up pussies! Knock it off!

G I: *(Still carried away)* Moral decay with L B J!

SERGEANT: *(Shoving him)* Knock it off, you traitor. You're talking about my President. I love my President. *(Talking at the* G I*)* I love our President. If this guy would talk like I know he can talk instead of all this peace, hope and stop and end war talk, I just know he could put them all down. We're not much more than fleas—so why don't we talk like fleas? Why doesn't this guy talk to them like I know he could? All his speech writers get in between him and us. Our peace Pope! Pope Pipe! I mean if our President can scratch his balls in public and those fancy pants in London don't like it, I say we learned it from them. They ain't so far up since Shakespeare!

*(*G I *he's been haranguing pushes him away gently and points him toward another couple.)*

G I: Tell them. Tell them.

SERGEANT: *(Weaving over to the next couple)* I think this guy is really in touch with the people.

(All the actors stop dancing in couples and become aspects of the SERGEANT*'s nightmare. They alternately accuse and attack him with images that have occurred throughout the play—drill, salutes, pushups, bayonetting, the* MADONNA, JERRY*'s death, Vietnamese mothers. The scene should become phantasmagoric.)*

SERGEANT: He knows what's happening. But the Eastern King Makers got their prejudice out for him! Poor bastard, it's more important that he should cut his nails right than he should make peace in the world. *(He collars another couple.)* Right now we're in the grips of the most prejudiced war we've ever fought. The Jews are mad that we're finally fighting for a minority *before* the genocide; they don't want no fights unless it's for them. This here minority ain't Western European; they's our little yellow-skinned brothers with slant eyes and too small to tote our guns. They think it's more important that that guy in the White House learn to eat lung under glass. I say warm yer spareribs! *(He starts to chant.)* Get on with the war!

(Everyone picks it up and chants "Get on with the war." They chant and dance to a terrific pitch, then silence.)

SERGEANT: Get on with this war-and-win it! I say take it out. Take it out and let's see how long it is against Mao Tse! Take it out! Take it out! Remove it! I love our President. I love our President. *(To* SAIGON SALLY*)* I love our President!

SALLY: *(Trying to calm him. He collapses into her arms.)* Sure you do, baby.

G I: Sing us another song, Sal.

SALLY: Sure I will, baby. *(Embracing* SERGEANT*)* Come on, baby. You had yourself quite a blow.

G I: Come on and sing us another one, Sal.

SALLY: *(Pulling the clumsy* SERGEANT *to her and talking directly to him)*
Sure I will, baby. Dance with me?

(As she sings, the other couples dance slowly and lovingly.)

SALLY: Close your eyes and dance awhile,
Close your eyes and kiss my neck,
Just relax, you'll get the hang,
Close your eyes and kiss my chin,
Honey, relax, put down that gin.

Close your eyes and dance awhile,
Close your eyes and kiss my neck,
Just relax, you'll get the hang,
Close your eyes and kiss my chin,
Honey, relax, put down that gin.

Close your eyes and dance awhile,
Dance awhile, dance awhile,
Close your eyes and dance awhile,
Dance awhile, dance awhile.
That's the way,
That's the style,
Close your eyes and dance awhile,
Now, kiss my chin.

(Giant explosion. The bar is blown to bits. The explosion reverberates and repeats. As it begins to die down we see all the bodies exploding to the pulse of the sound. This is done in slow motion. As the sound dies away we see everyone in a clustered death struggle. The bodies are massed together center stage, tangled and flailing in slow motion. They stab one another, shoot one another, and choke one another as they fall in a heap to the floor. All sound has stopped. There is no sound of the death struggle. When all are dead they are in a tangled circle on the floor, the reverse of the beautiful circle of the opening image. There is silence for the count of ten. Then flat, emotionless voices are heard saying the following lines. The lines must not be said with any personal attitude and should overlap. The director should assign the lines to the actors.)

Doves.War. Take away. Treasure lost. Lost our treasure. Lose our treasure. Spend all our natural resources. Cannon fodder. The cost is high. And our boys our dollars. Dollars beget dollars but boys don't come back. My boy, my boy. Come back. Bring him back. Bring back my boy. Dear God. Dear God. Hear me you bloody blessed and deadening God. Hear me dear God. Hear my prayer dearest God. I will give all my dollars to bring my boy back home again. All my dollars. Let him come home again. I give all. All all all my dollars. I give all my dollars. Let him come home once again. Blow it up. Blow it. Blow the whites of his frigging eyes to kingdom come again. Blow the rice right out of his gut. Gut his gut. Gut to gut. Butt to butt. Crack his nuts. Destroy his blood. Spill blood. Show your love by spilling your blood. The death ship. Grenade. Blow. Bullet. Bayonet. Knife. Cut. Slash open his neck or lay down yours. Move it shithead. Get the lead out dickhead. Come on girls lift up your skirts and wiggle your way to glory. Wiggle your way. Wiggle your ass. Fart that gas and putt your butt to glory. Bug out you scab. Bug out. Bugged Buggest. Bugged. A point of no return. No return. A point. There is a point somewhere. There is a point where all the points jab the head of the angel. Super super sonic blades. Travel super. Argue freedom. Happy days honey. Up yours bunny. Funny you used to be so sunny. I fought for you upstairs. Loony tunes. Hi ya doc! Humphrey's voyage of reassurance. But Gandhi's dead. Chocolate soda. Two scoops. Big Daddy Flew Out. To give us a handout. Out. Out. Oops there goes my arm again. There goes my head again. Shooting through the Blue Yonder my boys. Oops there went the green of my eyes and the glow of my heart. Oops there went my belly into the gully. Remember me to Mom boys. And have another shave. When you get back think of me boys. Think of me. Oops there went my legs again. The sun also rises but not my cock. Goodbye to the thunder of the Sun. You son-of-a-bitch. Goodbye dickheads of the world. Who needs me. Who needs this. Who needs war. Who needs this shit. I'm in the shit. Who needs me. Who. Who needs. Who needs. Who.

(Then the entire company says the following together and the heap should pulse like a giant beating heart.)

COMPANY: WHO WHO WHO WHO WHO WHO WHO WHO WHO WHO—!

(As the last line dies away there is silence for a count of twenty. Then one by one the actors rise. They must do so in extreme slow motion as if coming back from a long distance. They are fragile. They are angels. They are beautiful. One by one they stand. One by one they enter the audience. Each chooses an audience member and touches his hand, head, face, hair. Look and touch. Look and touch. A celebration of presence. They go among the audience until every actor has left the stage Then as the song begins they leave the auditorium. In no way should the actors communicate superiority. They must communicate a wonder and gift of being actually alive together with the audience at that moment.)

Far across the Southern Sea
Is a land where Viets rock.
Here every morning you can see
The Viets roll.

When the bombs fall
The Viets rock and rock.
When the napalm bursts
Then the Viets roll.

At the sound of jets
The Viets rock and rock.

When the tracers flash
Then the Viets roll.

Rock and roll, rock and roll
How the sweet Viets
Love to rock and roll.
Those dear little Viets
Love our rock and roll.

Do the Viet Rock,
Watch that Viet roll.
Do the Viet Rock,
Watch that Viet roll.
That's the way the Viets rock,
All the way the Viets roll.
Rock and roll, rock and roll,
Do the Viet Rock.

END OF PLAY

ALTERNATE SCENE

To be used in place of or in addition to final crawling scene

(Begin after JOE*'s speech cue: "I'll fight for you guys any day of the week. You're good people. The best!")*

(Abrupt transition. All actors are now V-C. A Viet Cong stronghold. A local tribunal is present. It is presided over by the local V-C COMMANDER*. At his side sits his beautiful Vietnamese* MISTRESS*. The* COMMANDER *reaches over and squeezes his mistress's breast. She pretends to sigh. But her eyes are apprehensive. He pulls her to him and leans on her voluptuously. He turns and calls to a guard.)*

COMMANDER: Bring in the Uncle Sam criminal.

*(*SOLDIER*, speaking gibberish, pushes in one of our* G IS*. He's tied to a stake at his back; there is writing on the stake. It isn't a stationary stake, but runs only down as far as his hips.)*

COMMANDER: Good morning, barbarian mafia. It is time for you to leave our lovely world. Do you have anything to say before you depart?

G I: *(Looks briefly at girl and we see something flash between them)* Allen, Seth, Private First Class, 1-1-3-3-4-5-6-7-9-G-H-T, U S Army.

COMMANDER: I repeat, this is your last sunrise. You are to die for the blood of our heroic brother that was shed in Saigon this time yesterday morning. A wanton murder by criminal puppets of the Jesse James, U S Uncle Sam imperialist invaders. Is there nothing you want left hanging on our air waves?

G I: *(Bravely)* Allen, Seth, Private First Class, 1-1-3-3-4-5-6-7-9-G-H-T, U S Army.

COMMANDER: Billy Barbarian the Kid Machine! *(He spits at G I, then kisses and fondles his* MISTRESS *and looks to see the effect on the soldier.)* Are you sure there isn't something you'd like to whisper. A sweet nightingale song, perhaps, into a lotus ear?

G I: Allen, Seth, Private First Class, 1-1-3-3-4-5-6-7-9-G-H-T, U S Army.

COMMANDER: *(Looks at his watch)* I've indulged you enough, Ma Rainey vicious mad-dog-killer of trees and huts. Parade the criminal.

(Two V-C parade the G I *around the village, dragging and kicking him. Villagers throw dirt and spit on him. One demented villager almost foams at the mouth while punching and scratching at the* G I*, babbling in gibberish and getting more and*

more excited. As the violence mounts, the MISTRESS *of the* COMMANDER *begins to perspire and inadvertently clutches the arm of her master. He notices it.)*

COMMANDER: *(He gestures toward the excited, demented* V-C.*)* Come. *(To* G I*)* His entire family was burned before his eyes from your napalm Baby Face Nelson. Come, little one. *(To demented* V-C.*)* You can have revenge. Which part of this pig do you want to hang from a pole outside your cave? Take your time, choose with care. Only one piece. There isn't enough of this skinny Capone to go around.

(The V-C, *nearly drooling with glee, looks all over the* G I. *First he grabs a thumb, then an ear, a nose, his tongue. He shakes his head, finally points to* G I*'s chest where his heart would be.)*

COMMANDER: Heart?

(The MISTRESS *lets a little cry escape her. The* COMMANDER *turns and grabs her and twists her arm.)*

COMMANDER: Now I know where you've been stealing when the moon is high. If you've lifted your slippers heavenward for him you can now share his fate.

(He pushes her out into the clearing and she bumps into SETH. *He tries to show no emotion but is clearly distressed.)*

COMMANDER: Now she's close enough for you to whisper into her traitorous ear.

G I: You're unjust.

COMMANDER: Don't tell me what I am, Legs Diamond. *(He carefully aims at the girl.)* Kneel.

MISTRESS: *(Kneeling)* Yes, my lord.

COMMANDER: Put your head to the earth of your ancestors.

MISTRESS: *(Touching ground with her head)* Yes, my lord.

COMMANDER: *(Watching* G I *all the time, he walks slowly to the girl and puts the barrel of the gun against the back of her neck. To* SETH*)* Is there something you wanted to say now?

G I: You're making a mistake.

COMMANDER: It is you who have made the mistake.

(He fires the gun into the girl's head and she falls at the feet of the G I. *He flinches and tries not to gasp.)*

COMMANDER: It is your turn. You have one more chance to give information to save your corrupt skin.

G I: Allen, Seth, Private First Class...

COMMANDER: Little one. Would you like the honor?

(He brings the demented V-C *to his side.)*

COMMANDER: Come, I'll help you hold the gun. We'll shoot him bit by bit.

(The little one, foaming and gurgling, leaps to the COMMANDER. *Together they get the gun pointed at* SETH.*)*

COMMANDER: First his belly *(Bang)* Good. Good. Now a shot for each shoulder *(Bang, bang)* Excellent. Now his pee pee *(Bang)* Good.

G I: *(Listing, but still trying to stand tall)* Allen, Seth, Private First Class...

COMMANDER: No, no, little one. Don't aim for the heart. That's for your very own. The nose. No. The eyes? One for each of the ugly round Yankee eyes. Two for you, round eyes *(Bang, bang)*

V-C: *(Jumps up and down with glee and runs to body, chops at the chest and pulls out the heart and sucks on the stringy arteries)* Ummmmmmm ymmmmmmm...

COMMANDER: Mine their bodies with grenade booby traps. Leave them on the trail for the next G I platoon to stumble over.

(He grabs another woman and fondles and kisses her and says sweet things while bodies are rigged and light fades.)

(Song: Men Die Young *to be placed here instead of after Buddhist funeral.)*